jewelry from nature

Thames & Hudson

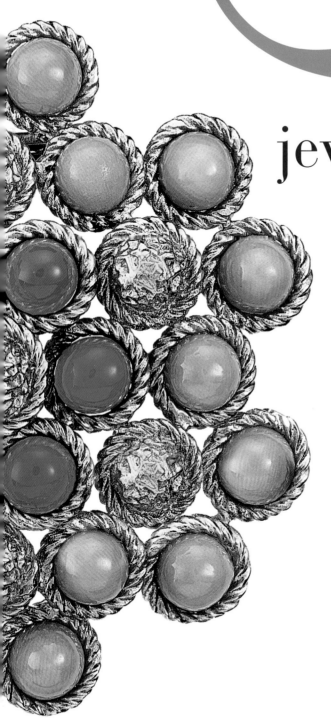

jewelryfromnature

*Amber Coral Horn Ivory Pearls Shell
Tortoiseshell Wood Exotica*

Ruth Peltason

With over 350 colour illustrations

Contents

Introduction

The Living Jeweled Kingdom

*b*lame it on Art Nouveau. Blame it on Torre del Greco and Pompeii. Blame it on Howard Carter, Queen Victoria and René Lalique. Call it a coup d'état, although change was neither limited to one country nor one specific time: over recent centuries a gradual revolution has occurred in the way the best jewelry firms and makers looked at what jewelry *could* be. By the mid-1800s precious stones – think diamonds and emeralds – were eased from their starring roles to make way for their understudies: coral, shell cameo and lava jewelry became a thriving business in southern Italy, tortoiseshell and jet were primarily used for mourning jewelry in England, and in Europe and America pearls were being made into the finest necklaces, brooches and earrings. A pattern began to emerge: *inherent value*, that telltale phrase of Art Nouveau jewelry indicating a new emphasis on underused and utilitarian materials, could be applied more broadly as a way of understanding a new, primary and lasting emphasis on living materials in jewelry.

Consider a diamond, for it is beautiful, and within its finely faceted body all the colours we might possibly imagine can be gleaned. But it lacks one property common to, say, shells and amber, even something as quotidian as horn and ivory: it has never been *alive*. The coral that grows in sea beds, the tortoise that ever so slowly crawls through grasses, the amber that once formed drop by golden drop from tree resin, even the butterflies that float on currents of air share a unique language – life. No mineral, regardless how dazzling or rare, can claim this impermanence of being, the essence of our own mortality. The *living* jeweled kingdom draws from nature – those creatures that live on land, dwell in water, or fly through the air.

As I began to consider what is living jewelry, I wondered whether such materials might form a valid way of thinking about important jewelry, apart from the usual gemstone giants such as diamonds or rubies. The answers, surprisingly, are supported by hundreds of superb pieces. One evening I got to talking over dinner with a friend of mine, Daphne Lingon, a jewelry specialist at Christie's, about some wood jewelry we both admired, and it occurred to us that we'd never seen a book that surveyed the use of organic, living materials in jewelry. We started to list jewelers we could think of over the past two hundred years or so who have

worked with coral, or horn, or ivory, not to mention something as ubiquitous but taxonomically diverse as pearls. The result of our so-called name game was staggering: every major jeweler in the Western world could be accounted for, along with those equally talented but often anonymous Georgians and Victorians. The ABC of names read like a Who's Who of Great Jewelers, among them older, established houses such as Bulgari, Cartier, Boucheron, Van Cleef & Arpels, Tiffany & Co., Mauboussin, Lacloche Frères, Nardi, Harry Winston; historically important designers, including Lalique, Castellani, Suzanne Belperron, Verdura, Schlumberger, Raymond Templier, Boivin; modern and contemporary designers including David Webb, Donald Claflin, JAR, Andrew Grima, William Spratling, Marguerite Stix, James de Givenchy, Patricia Von Musulin, Ted Muehling, Elsa Peretti, Noma Copley, Kiff Slemmons. The lists are long, the quality superb.

And what exactly were these materials? I came to think of them as *living* or *natural*, words that in the context of jewelry beg for discussion and debate. Aren't minerals natural? Well, yes, which would mean that precious stones such as diamonds, emeralds and sapphires should be considered. But then again, perhaps not, because what I truly mean are those materials whose *origins were as living creatures*, such as coral and shells, or as part of a living creature, such as pearls, the horns or antlers of a mammal, the mottled shell of a tortoise. Moreover, whereas gemstones have the advantage of durability, organic materials are the 'weaker sex' of the jeweler's world, being more dependent on oxygen and nourishment, and ultimately more fragile. Eventually I settled on a list that felt reasonably definitive (or something I could tolerably defend): amber, coral, horn, ivory, pearls, shell, tortoiseshell and wood. To which I added a slew of what nowadays constitutes more exotic materials, such as scarab beetles, tiger claws, stag's teeth, bog oak, hair, even feathers – examples of the latter truly exquisite, though the birds were sadly exploited in their day.

In fact, when considering this jewelry, the inevitable subject of protection of living species met the nature-loving pacifist in me. Although I don't condone harming an animal for the sake of beauty, my role here is curator, not censor. I view all of these works – a scarab necklace, an ivory brooch – in terms of their historical value and what they add to our understanding of material culture

at a given time. Today, mammoth ivory is used instead of elephant tusk ivory; tortoiseshell and coral are protected; and we would all prefer to watch the flight of a hummingbird rather than see it as taxidermy for brooches or millinery.

As curator, then, there was the matter of honing my criteria for selecting works. For instance, how to choose among hundreds, no, thousands, of items made with pearls, surely the most widely used of the materials I'd chosen to be featured. Coral was also a material that posed a challenge because so many examples of fine jewelry are made with coral. Ultimately, I opted for three guidelines in selecting objects: Essence, Importance and Freshness.

With regard to *essence*, I valued those pieces in which the material was essential to the impact or design. Elementary in this regard is Andrew Grima's featherweight but enormous chunky amber pendant, complete with a little fly forever suspended in its resin body. Another striking example is a large crab carved from coral and set as a ring by the uniquely talented Monica Rossi from Italy, the mollusk so lifelike it seems vaguely predatory. In the nineteenth century it applies to the wildly odd baroque pearls used to form figural brooches, among them swans or turtles or birds, including a dazzling lyrebird. I defined *importance* as objects meaningful or historically significant to the canon or the maker, such as Lalique's luminous Art Nouveau horn and pearl diadem; Van Cleef & Arpels's grape cluster brooch of natural pearls made circa 1915; Cartier's Art Deco coral dragon bangles. *Freshness* allowed me to select objects that expressed originality and piquant design rather than the weight of history or reputation. Here I ranged more widely and more freely over recent years, so there is Ted Muehling's Queen Anne's Lace pin, a delicately pocked gold disk with keshi pearls embedded like tiny blossoms; an assortment of ivory bangles and cuffs by Patricia Von Musulin that look more like miniature architectural dwellings or artisanal meringues than jewelry; a butterfly-and-pigment necklace by Jennifer Trask, which in one click of the clasp joins the nineteenth century with our own.

The overall time period for the objects shown here ranges from the early 1800s to the present, from the late Georgian era to now, which for lack of a better word is called contemporary. Along the way are works that hail from important

design periods – among them Victorian, Arts & Crafts, Art Nouveau, Belle Epoque, Edwardian, Art Deco and Retro.

Cuff bangle, probably by Suzanne Belperron, French, c. 1940 Cultured pearls and 18K gold

I hope that these three concepts – essence, importance and freshness – allow enough latitude to sneak in a fourth one, an *x* factor, which is how jewelry sparks our imagination and touches our soul. This is where the appeal of jewelry moves out of the shop window or museum and into our hearts, where I believe a passion for jewelry begins. Cherishing jewelry is something that first occurs at home, when one is just a girl. An unspoken threshold is crossed when a young girl is shown her mother's or her grandmother's jewelry or receives her first piece of 'real' jewelry. For me it was a thin gold ring with a caramel-coloured topaz, my birthstone, given to me by my great-grandmother when I was five, followed some time later by the evolving, built-in sentiment of a silver charm bracelet from my parents. These gifts – and the looking and sharing of stories about family jewelry – are each stamped with the most timeless of hallmarks: Meaning and Memory. Even the occasional piece of jewelry that I've lost (including that diminutive topaz ring!), is forever secure in my mind: the *memory* of jewelry given to me remains vibrant and its *meaning*, if anything, is even greater today. I suspect that this is true for each of us, that our own things, or those belonging to others, become talismans, a way of connecting history with personal ownership. Hence that more grown-up word, *provenance*, played a role in my selection from the living jeweled kingdom, including a coral and diamond star-shaped brooch created by Diana Vreeland from a necklace owned by her mother; a pearl necklace given by President Ulysses Grant to his wife; the Peregrina pearl necklace, today owned by Elizabeth Taylor but over the centuries worn on the royal necks of queens in Spanish and French courts.

The life force that courses through these jeweled works – a coral Buddha brooch of great merriment and calm; amber earrings which are glowing orbs of light by JAR; an array of embellished wood and lacquer butterfly brooches from Van Cleef & Arpels – has given me great joy to discover. Amber, coral, horn, ivory, pearls, shell, tortoiseshell and wood – the foot soldiers of this quiet revolution in jewelry – are each presented here, dressed in their proudest best.

1.

Amber,
History Preserved

W hat a pity that amber is underappreciated or little known today, for it is surely one of the distinguished senior members among the world of organic materials, with a lineage dating back some 300 million years. Amber clues us in to how we lived (or rather, how small insects and flowering species lived and where); it features in mythology; and has been used as a medicinal by some cultures. As a preservative it is sine qua non. It is, one could say, a material with a 'past'.

Amber ear clip,
by JAR,
American,
late 20th century

Like a message in a bottle, this past is amber's great gift in our understanding of evolution, its unique substance harbouring traces of both fauna and flora millions of years old. In 1996, for example, our knowledge expanded when a piece of amber was found enclosing three intact flowers. The source was probably an oak tree, and the amber dated to a period 90 million years ago, when dinosaurs still roamed the world. This one single discovery – just three tiny flowers – changed our thinking on the origin of flowering plants, all thanks to the miraculous preserving power of amber.

Age and amber have a natural affinity, and aside from its important contributions to science, amber has chiefly been used for adornment. The oldest amber, which dates to the Cretaceous period (145 to 65 million years ago), is too brittle for jewelry; the best amber for use in jewelry is from the Tertiary period (65 million years ago to the present), principally from the eastern shores of the Baltic Sea, especially near the Samland Peninsula. (Remarkably this one peninsula, some 400 square miles, yields 90 per cent of European amber.) Geographically this includes areas around Poland, parts of Sweden and Denmark, Russia and Estonia. Amber has flowed into riverbeds and seas across the continents, from the upper reaches of Western Europe down into France, Austria and Italy (Sicilian amber is noteworthy), parts of North America (New Jersey is rich with amber deposits), the Dominican Republic (the second oldest source for amber, 25 to 15 million years old, and second to Baltic amber), Asia, the Middle East and Japan.

This ancient organic is fossilized tree resin from conifers and pines, as well as some tropical trees. This thick resin acted like an airtight bandage when a tree limb broke or was invaded by, say, bark beetles; the tree would release its sticky substance to staunch the wound, thereby sealing the wood from further damage. But woe to the slow-moving insect or lizard who was trapped in the amber resin substance before it hardened – its fate sealed for an eternity.

As these ancient trees rotted, they were preserved in sediment at the bottom of riverbeds, carried downstream and into vast bodies of water. Amber doesn't actually float, though it is lighter than seawater and was sometimes seen bobbing near the surface of the Baltic Sea, where fishermen would gather it in large nets, hence its English nickname of 'scooping stone'.

Enviably, amber doesn't show its age, which automatically reflects well upon any woman wearing a necklace whose beads are millions of years old. A stylish woman in nineteenth-century Europe or America might well have been wearing amber beads 65 or 45 million years old. In the twentieth century, two jewelers in particular, Andrew Grima and Gilbert Albert, accorded the seat of honour to this ancient resin by privileging it as a pendant in its most natural, untouched form. Grima, who was born in Rome and trained in London, had an abiding respect for nature, which shows in his chunky amber pendant on page 17. His contemporary, Swiss-born Albert, similarly exalted amber's natural state, though he couldn't resist adding a few fanciful flourishes in gold and a cultured pearl, page 17.

Preservation and procreation: honouring the past yet looking to the future – isn't this the underlying foundation of every great civilization? As for the stingless bees or tiny flies found in amber, look closely at that pendant made by Andrew Grima. Bzzzzzzz...

Nothing can surpass the exquisite colours of this rainbow-hued Sicilian amber — nothing but the Sicilian sunset itself. THE NATIONAL OBSERVER, c. 1900

William Arnold Buffum:
An Ardour for Amber

One of the great amber collectors was William Arnold Buffum, who wrote the now-classic book on the subject, *Tears of the Heliades, or Amber as a Gem*, published in London, 1898. Like many Americans of his day, William Arnold Buffum made the Grand Tour of Europe and became both connoisseur and collector, eventually donating much of his collection to the Museum of Fine Arts in his hometown of Boston. As he wrote in the book's introduction, 'I have succeeded in making a notable collection of amber specimens from different countries, and of art-works of this incomparable substance.' He refers to amber as being 'curious and captivating', and citing his ambition to clear up 'the amber mystery', that is, both its origins and its age. Happily for us, Buffum the researcher was compatible with Buffum the cognoscente: the amber demi-parure in the archaeological revival style seen on pages 14–15 was commissioned by Buffum, and not only showed off the quality amber he collected but also the revived interest in jewelry at that time in Greek, Roman and Etruscan styles.

Amber girandole ear pendants,

Sicilian, c. 19th century

Amber and silver

According to Professor David Grimaldi,
'Amber is entirely organic; its composition
from the original resin has changed little
over millions of years.'

Castellani: The Masters of Archaeological Revival Jewelry

Fate, fortune and fame came to rest squarely on the three-generation shoulders of the Castellani family. *Fate* because the eldest member, Fortunato Pio, who had already set up shop in Rome in 1814, met Michelangelo Caetani, Duke of Sermoneta, a man of worldly interests and social connections with the entrepreneurial acumen to encourage Castellani Sr in reviving ancient forms in jewelry. *Fortune* because by the 1830s the firm was successfully producing archaeological jewelry and gaining exclusive entrée to such places as the newly opened Etruscan Regolini-Galassi tombs as well as a first-class private collection of antique jewelry which its designers studied and soon began producing themselves. By the 1840s, with sons Alessandro and Augusto, the Castellani firm had learned ancient techniques of working with gold and were making superb jewelry with intaglios and cameos, scarabs and, most significantly, micro-mosaics. Their name became synonymous with archaeological revival jewelry through two international exhibitions back to back (Florence in 1861 and London in 1862), resulting in that most elusive intangible many seek but few attain: *fame.*

Archaeological revival amber fringe necklace, ear pendants and brooch, possibly Castellani, Italian, c. 1880
Amber and gold

William Buffum commissioned this demi-parure based on a necklace worn by Galatea, a young Sicilian peasant he met while in Palestrina, just east of Rome. Buffum was dazzled by the amber colouring and tried to buy the necklace, but without success. Galatea wouldn't part with it. The original, which he named 'The Necklace of Galatea', had thirteen multi-coloured stones, whereas Buffum's consisted of seventeen caramel-hued stones, though in all other respects the two are identical. Buffum showed the Galatea necklace on the frontispiece of his Tears of the Heliades (1898).

We despair of ever imitating the ancient work perfectly…

CASTELLANI

Amber sautoir, c. 1910–20
Amber beads

*Queen Alexandra is frequently
credited with popularizing the sautoir
– a long necklace, typically
40 inches (1 metre), often with
a pendant or tassel.*

Caught in Amber, the Forever Fossil

Flora and fauna, that alliterative expression so beloved by the naturalist, have been on display for literally millions of years for those who look deeply into the honeyed hues of amber. What can you see? Insects, chiefly – among them flies, ants, pseudoscorpions, spiders, mosquitoes, wasps and bees. Flora, too, such as liverwort, oak leaf and oak flowers, conifer and pine needles. It's these hard animal skeletons or shells and woody plant materials that leave such helpful fossil remains for paleontologists. Imagine that in these telling amber droplets scientists can claim with near certainty the existence of the oldest bee, the stingless bee (*Trigona prisca*), 65 to 80 million years ago, and the oldest mushroom, *Archaeomarasmius leggetti*, from 90 to 94 million years ago. Both were found in New Jersey, which might surprise those who put Baltic amber on a jeweled pedestal.

Amber necklace,

by Andrew Grima, English, c. 1960–70

Amber, diamonds and 18K gold

This amber chunk may look heavy, but in fact like all amber it is surprisingly lightweight. Grima was enchanted with natural materials, and on this occasion he was able to preserve amber's fluid-like form as well as the very small insect trapped for all eternity within the resin body.

Amber pendant and chain,

by Gilbert Albert, Swiss, c. 1970s

Amber, cultured pearl and 18K gold

As with so much well-made jewelry, this pendant also converts into a necklace and bracelet.

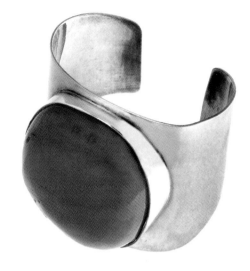

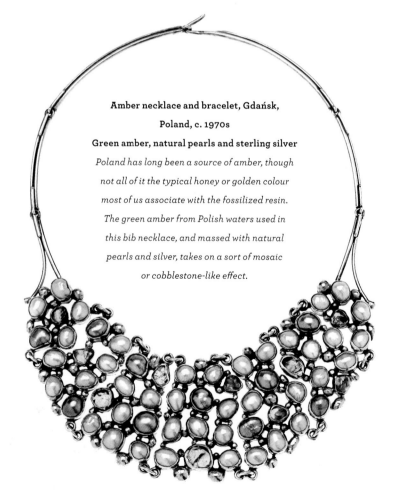

**Amber necklace and bracelet, Gdańsk,
Poland, c. 1970s**

Green amber, natural pearls and sterling silver

*Poland has long been a source of amber, though
not all of it the typical honey or golden colour
most of us associate with the fossilized resin.
The green amber from Polish waters used in
this bib necklace, and massed with natural
pearls and silver, takes on a sort of mosaic
or cobblestone-like effect.*

Amber cuff, Finnish, c. 1971
Amber and silver

*Given Finland's location, the amber used in this
cuff may have come from one of the Western
European countries bordering the Baltic Sea,
the chief source of quality amber. By 1970, the
interest in clean design and emphasis on natural
materials was evident in Scandinavia. Finland,
in particular, was also the birthplace
of Marimekko and designers such as
Alvar Aalto, Tapio Wirkkala and Iittala.*

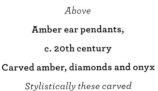

Above

Amber ear pendants,

c. 20th century

Carved amber, diamonds and onyx

*Stylistically these carved
amber ear pendants
show an Asian influence.*

Left

Amber ear pendants,

20th century

Amber, cultured pearls, diamonds and gold

*It's unusual to find modern jewelry made with
amber, yet the designer of this set was clever
in combining it with pearls. The result is
unexpected yet refreshing.*

Amber ear clips, by JAR,
American, late 20th century
Carved amber and 18K gold

Jewelry made by JAR always has that 'je ne sais
quoi' quality about it. The use of stippling over
the amber surface gives added texture
and dimensionality to the commanding
simplicity of these orbs.

Amber bead necklace,
by Rebecca Koven, Canadian, 2008
Faceted amber and 22K gold beads

The amber is from the Baltic region, the much-
heralded source of the best amber for jewelry,
and the beads are each hand-faceted.

Amber and ebony pendant necklace,
by Patricia Von Musulin, American, c. 2000
Amber and hand-carved ebony beads
The Greek word for amber is elektron,
meaning sun, which describes the way this
amber radiates such brilliance. The night
(the ebony beads) and day effect (the amber)
gives exotic appeal to this overly large necklace.

A Six-Ton Beauty Carved in Amber

What has been called 'the eighth wonder of the world' abounded in six tons of amber and precious stones, floor inlay of exotic woods, amber panels covering 180 square feet (17 square metres), and glowed with the illumination of more than 550 candles. As private rooms in palatial residences go, it rivalled the Hall of Mirrors in Versailles, a 220-foot-long (67-metres) gallery with 357 mirrors. The Amber Room was indeed a magnificent sight: 100,000 carved pieces of amber – coats of arms, inlay of land-scapes and allegorical scenes, and monograms – mounted on twenty-two panels, and assembled in 1770 in one of the grand chambers of the Catherine Palace, near St Petersburg. It began as a gift from the King of Prussia to Peter the Great in 1716, cementing an alliance between Russia and Prussia – and ended in plunder by the Nazis during World War II, whose 'reclamation' the rest of the world saw purely as theft. Among the many art treasures looted by the Nazis, this one has remained a total mystery: not one of the amber-encrusted panels has been seen since. But in 2003, at great effort and expense, a full replica was completed and installed once again in the Catherine Palace, in time for the 300th anniversary of the founding of St Petersburg.

Amber ear pendants,
by Ted Muehling, American, 2009
Hand-carved amber and 14K gold

You can get a lot of power out of form that's a centimetre long…. That one-centimetre piece does two things. It's a bit of punctuation and it might draw someone toward you. TED MUEHLING

The Seahorse is Not a Horse

Scientific information on the seahorse abounds with unusual facts. First of all, the seahorse is a fish, belonging to the genus *Hippocampus*, from the Greek *hippos* for horse and *kampos* for sea monster. Unlike most of their fellow fish, the seahorse is monogamous and mates for life (couples swim in pairs, tail linked to tail, a fishlike way of holding hands). This upright swimmer bobs about in tropical and temperate waters all over the world (coral reefs are a favourite), and ranges in size from one-sixth of an inch to 14 inches (0.5 cm–35 cm). Mating takes place under a full moon to a soft symphony of sound produced by the romancing seahorses. Because the female deposits her eggs into the male's pouch, which he fertilizes internally, the male seahorse is the only male on earth that produces babies. Once the eggs hatch, 'Papa' releases his miniature babes into the water; by the time they're two weeks old, newborn seahorses consume from 3,000 to 4,000 brine shrimp a day. As far as looks go, they're a winning composite of many other creatures: they have the head of a horse, the pouch of a kangaroo, the prehensile tail of a monkey, and like chameleons they can change colour to blend with their surroundings.

What works against them? They are utterly adorable, which makes them vulnerable as souvenirs and pets, and they're used in some Asian medicines. Thankfully, they have been officially protected since 2004.

Seahorse brooch,
by Elizabeth Gage, British, 2005
Carved amber, citrine and 18K gold
In the world of Elizabeth Gage, the
appeal of nature recurs in her various brooches
and necklaces, beginning with the first piece
of jewelry she made, in 1964 – a butterfly
out of silver. Many years later this seahorse came
along, the amber standing in for the golds
and yellows seen among the variable colours
of this endearing aquatic creature.

C

2.

Coral,
The 'Red Gold' of the Sea

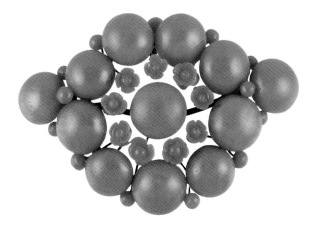

What is it about coral that makes it so ardently modern? Even a brooch from the mid-1800s, made up of a dozen or so coral beads, somehow looks fresh, tangy, like the perfect orange. Of course coral isn't quite orange, but neither is it red: if coral were a sibling in a family you'd call it the 'pleaser', for there is something soothing and appealing about its merry impact. It neither screams nor retreats: its presence is both welcoming and warming. Perhaps this explains its timeless appeal, for it has been worked to great effect by the Victorians as well as such twentieth-century jewelry stars as David Webb (his chimera bangle is a mythic journey in itself) and Cartier, who made Art Deco objects replete with layers of myth and meaning, the likes of which have never been surpassed for their originality and execution.

Coral brooch, c. 1860

The coral most frequently used for jewelry comes from the genus *Corallium*, what the jewelry trade refers to as 'precious coral'. And while the colour range includes the extremes white and black (the rarer of the two), the most common stops along the coral colour bar tend to be pale pink, sometimes referred to as angel skin, peach, and orange-red. The deeply red coral, *C. rubrum*, is the most ubiquitous coral used for jewelry, and its principal home for centuries is one of the world's most enchanting bodies of water, the Mediterranean. If coral spoke, its language would probably be Italian, for it has traditionally been most plentiful in the area called Torre del Greco, near Naples, where since around 1805 it has been harvested and carved, and also in Sardinia, sometimes described as the 'coral Riviera'. But coral's reach extends into the ocean, too, such as the Atlantic around the Strait of Gibraltar and in the Pacific around both Japan and Taiwan. But no matter what water it inhabits, this type of coral is a dedicated cave dweller, a shade seeker, and most happy when it can burrow into rocky walls or underwater ravines at depths of 30–1,000 feet (10–300 metres). Although this bonny coloured species looks like a shrub or miniature tree with limbs, coral is actually not a plant but an animal, a point accepted as fact only in the nineteenth century.

If you were to sit before a world map showing where coral has surfaced over the centuries in jewelry or been used for its religious or spiritual attributes, you'd find that coral is a natural point of connection between the East and the West. Perhaps this is a result of its rich red hue, which suggests power and allure, seduction and fertility, life force and health. Marco Polo, that great Venetian wanderer of the thirteenth century, included coral in the caravan of goods he hauled along the Silk Road, evidence of the gem's growing importance. And though its talismanic role can be traced back to prehistory, by the 1800s the Victorians were using coral in their jewelry to symbolize romance (love, marriage and fertility) and nature (a red rose was an especially popular motif). Coral has always been kind to the carver, and as the age of travel and the Grand Tour gained toehold, including tours of vast archaeological excavations worldwide, mythological motifs became fashionable for coral jewelry. The features of heralded Greek and Roman deities such as Zeus, Aphrodite, Bacchus, Psyche, Minerva and Poseidon began appearing on brooches, bracelets and necklaces, making the bejeweled lady of the late nineteenth century an attractive bearer of ancient history.

Once the twentieth century got under way, however, spells and potions and symbols of faith or fortitude were like yesterday's newspaper, matters of little consequence. Coral went from meaning to à la mode, above all in Paris, the birthplace of fashion and home to some of the greatest jewelry designers of all time – Cartier, Van Cleef & Arpels, Mauboussin, Fouquet, Lacloche Frères, Sterlé and Boivin. But this is not to overlook Italy, that other great creative hub of Europe, where the house of Bulgari has made grand contribution to the coral jewelry box. French and Italian designers ushered in the new century with coral jewelry that continues to set the highest standards for ingenuity, craftsmanship and style. So too have solo artists worldwide distinguished themselves working in coral, proof positive that this colourful stone has timeless appeal.

Previous page
Coral brooch, c. 1860
Coral beads and carved rosettes
What goes around comes around: When you loosen up the timelines of when things were made, you can see recurring concepts in every discipline: certainly in fashion, in graphic art and design, and in jewelry. This brooch, made some 150 years ago, continues to look current, and would be a happy companion piece to the Vreeland star brooch, page 36.

Coral archaeological revival ear pendants, c. 1870
Coral beads and drops, enamel and gold
By the latter part of the 1800s, wealthy Europeans and Americans were on the move – travelling, discovering foreign places, and revelling in whatever was newly unearthed. The influence of treasures from archaeological digs – especially Etruscan, Greek and Roman jewelry – ripped through Western culture: patterns on sterling silver and porcelain, carvings on furniture, textile designs, and of course jewelry, all took a page from the colourful past.

Coral archaeological revival necklace, ear pendants and brooch, Italian, c. 1850s
Carved coral and gold

This suite is revivalist in style, and laudatory in its salutation to the ever-thirsty Bacchus, Roman god of wine, also known as Dionysus to the Greeks.

Coral and gold archaeological revival brooch and ear pendants, Italian, 19th century
Carved coral ram's heads and gold wire

In ancient Greece, a ram's head was a potent symbol of fertility and power, and has long been depicted in jewelry, on pottery and on coins.

Coral Egyptian revival necklace, c. 1870
Carved coral, faience, enamel,
carnelian, moonstone, turquoise and gold

By the latter part of the nineteenth century, the interest in things Egyptian was buttressed by the construction of the Suez Canal (officially completed in November 1869), and by Auguste Mariette, whose excavation work in Egypt on behalf of the Louvre led, among other things, to the discovery of the Avenue of the Sphinxes and the foundation of the Egyptian Museum in Cairo in 1858. This necklace bears the telltale motifs of the Egyptian revival: the ram heads, suggesting power and fertility, and the scarab, sacred symbol of life and good fortune.
For a bit of film trivia, Meryl Streep as Miranda Priestly wore this necklace in The Devil Wears Prada *(2006).*

'The Most Complete Collection of Fine Coral Work in the World'

They were jewelers par excellence in London of the late nineteenth century. The Phillips Brothers, makers of this striking coral tiara, were important goldsmiths and jewelers and the leading supplier of coral goods in London. At the Paris International Exhibition of 1867 they won a gold medal, and in 1870, they claimed their universal dominance in an advertisement stating that theirs was 'the most complete collection of fine coral work in the world'. Robert Phillips, the dominant partner and considered the more gifted of the brothers, received the Order of the Crown of Italy for his services to the coral industry in Naples. The firm also held a royal warrant as jewelers to Albert Edward, Prince of Wales, later Edward VII, which they conveyed through the plumed mark – the Prince of Wales feathers – gracing their shop front on Cockspur Street. Like many jewelers of the time, their work was revivalist in manner, its motifs and inspiration drawn from objects they saw in the various museums, antique shops and galleries they visited.

**Art Nouveau coral pendant brooch,
by LeBolt & Co., American, c. 1905–10
Gold, coral and diamonds**

A fancy curled 'L' beside an upright lion was the hallmark of this Arts & Crafts jeweler and silversmith. LeBolt was established in Chicago in 1899, and by 1903 had opened a second American location on the fashionable block of Fifth Avenue and West Twenty-third Street in New York. The glories of this particular piece are its size – 3½ inches (8.9 cm) high, the only piece of this scale by LeBolt – and that it's entirely handmade. The proud owner would have worn it on a high collar or as what was quaintly called a corsage ornament, a large piece of jewelry that was typically pinned between a woman's décolletage and her waist.

**Coral tiara, by the Phillips Brothers,
English, c. late 1800s
Branch coral and beads, gilt metal**

Not the blood, sweat and tears from a crown of thorns, but a crown of coral branches and berries, which extends in a near circle, set on a gilt metal frame.

Coral brooch, by Cartier, French, late 1930s
Carved coral head, diamonds, emeralds, black enamel, platinum and 18K gold

The house of Cartier has a long association with the panther, from as early as 1914 when the sleek beast appeared on a wristwatch and more significantly in 1948 when the Duke of Windsor commissioned a pendant for his wife featuring a panther in gold. The rest, as the saying goes, 'is history'.

Above right
Art Deco carved coral amphora ear pendants, by Cartier, French, c. 1925
Carved coral amphoras, diamonds, emerald beads and platinum

Cartier was deep into revivalist jewelry around this time, with amphoras an important motif in their collection. The ancient history of amphoras dates back to the fifteenth century BC.

Art Deco coral bracelet, c. 1930
Coral beads, onyx, diamond and platinum

It's unfortunate that the maker of this bracelet is not known for it is an example of great workmanship designed with an unerring sense for balancing the circle and the square.

Châtelaine watch (front and back),
by Van Cleef & Arpels, French, c. 1922
Coral, onyx, brilliants and platinum

When the châtelaine, a decorative hook, came
into use in the eighteenth century it was an
accessory with a purpose. In lieu of pockets
(something yet to be considered necessary
for a lady), the châtelaine had on average
five chains from which were suspended such
practical bits as keys, sewing scissors, a
measuring tape, a watch, even a small notebook.
By the time this piece was made, however, both
the châtelaine and the watch were on the cusp of
a great change: the wristwatch for women had
arrived, and with it yet another opportunity for
a woman to wear something jeweled. But before
that happened, this stunning Art Deco tick-tock
was a glorious swan song.

'Paul Poiret à Paris'

Blame it on 'La Rose d'Iribe', Paul Poiret's 'It' dress of 1913. The Orientalist-inspired sheath with its bold aubergine colour was a classic textbook example of Poiret at the time, showcasing a textile designed by Raoul Dufy, a friend of Poiret's, and the all-over rose motif created by the multi-talented Paul Iribe. Poiret admired Iribe's pochoir printing technique, which resulted in flattened, simple line drawings in keeping with Poiret's own fashion silhouettes at the time, and had hired him to illustrate a limited-edition book of his clothes as well as an insignia. Iribe came up with the freely drawn rose, which became the designer's signature motif and appeared beside his name on his labels, 'Paul Poiret à Paris'. This gallant, headline-making Frenchman who clipped the corset and sheathed the body supple, and was given to grandness, both in his choice of colour and his sweeping liberation of women's fashion, may not have expected the rose to define his creations. But it was that rose which, in fashion's own garden, was accorded First Prize, and became a symbol for Paris and beauty. By the way, in 1911, Poiret, the King of Fashion and the Pasha of Paris, launched a perfume in his daughter's name, Rosine.

I am an artist, not a dressmaker. PAUL POIRET

Art Deco vanity case,
by Van Cleef & Arpels, French, 1926
Gold, enamel, coral, lapis lazuli, jade,
amethysts and diamonds
The carved roses here draw the eye to this
stunning Art Deco vanity case. Today's vanity
or cosmetic case is like a small suitcase, but
this slender beauty held only an evening's
necessities: some powder, a puff and lipstick.

Art Deco coral 'Poiret Rose' vanity case,
by Lacloche Frères, French, c. 1925
Carved coral rosettes, lapis lazuli, enamel,
diamonds, platinum and gold
Apart from Paul Poiret's telling rose motif on this
vanity case, there was a personal connection
between the couturier and the jeweler because
Poiret's nephew Nicolas Bongard at one time
worked for Lacloche Frères. (Bongard later
teamed up with Jean Schlumberger and moved
with him to New York to work for Tiffany.)
And Poiret's sister married René Boivin.
All of which makes this vanity case an 'all in
the family' affair, Parisian style.

Coral hand brooch,

by Cartier, French, c. 1937

Coral, diamond, black enamel and 18K gold

*A black rose, the 'flower of darkness', is freighted
with meaning, not all of it pleasant. Where a red
rose is a sign of love, the black rose can spell its
opposite: sorrow, hatred, even death. Stepping
back from this abyss, a black rose can less
dramatically suggest farewell.*

Coral rose,

by Cartier Paris, c. 1958

Coral, diamonds and platinum

*Roses have long been associated with love
– the standby arrangement, a dozen red
roses, is often given to express romance.
This Cartier rose is unusually large, which
begs the rhetorical question, 'Does size matter?'
Can love be measured?*

Coral hand and diamond brooch,

by Perry, American, c. 1950s

Coral, diamonds and gold

*Still the coral hand, but the diamonds have
replaced the black enamel for the rose and the
meaning may well be more upbeat and salutary.
A rose picked out in diamonds is always a piece
of jewelry to smile upon.*

Coral Buddha, c. 1900–1920

Carved coral Buddha head, diamonds and gold

What is it about a smiling Buddha that is so appealing – in this case a Buddha with the merriest diamond eyes? The entire visage, especially the full cheeks, expresses inner satisfaction and happiness, qualities not always easily attained!

Below

Coral brooch by Cartier, French?, late 1950s

Carved coral lizard and turtle, emeralds, diamonds, platinum and 18K gold

Symbolically, the turtle has represented heaven and earth, whereas the lizard figures more in dreams and soul searching. It's hard to say whether these creatures are locked in a duel, or represent the tangling of our thoughts and aspirations.

Coral brooch, by Cartier London, c. 1940

Carved coral, jade, natural pearls and diamonds

A showstopper of a piece with a strong Asian influence, made during the early years of World War II.

DV, Always in Style

It was a perfect alliance: Carmel Snow, the great editor of *Harper's Bazaar* and Diana Vreeland, her socialite-turned-fashion editor. The year was 1936, Americans were still pulling out of the Depression, and fashion, as a result, was struggling to get back on its pretty perch. In the space of time it took to write the headline, 'Why Don't You…?', fashion, *Harper's Bazaar* and Diana Vreeland had turned a couture corner. It wasn't just the quirkiness of DV's bons mots, it was the freshness, the loosening of rules, the sharp-as-a-tack instinct for the frugal and the fashionable, that won readers over to Diana Vreeland's highly amusing columns.

'Why Don't You…?':
· *wear, like the Duchess of Kent, three enormous diamond stars arranged in your hair in front?*
· *consider the chic of wearing bracelets high on the arm and try Lady Mendl's thick black leather bracelets, which she wears just above the elbow with a huge diamond bracelet at the wrist?*
· *wear a blue sapphire thistle in one ear and a ruby thistle in the other?*
· *try the lovely combination of tourmalines and pale rubies?*
· *take your old childhood coral beads and have them done up into big pins of flower designs on bracelets, studding the hole the cord went through with gold or a tiny diamond? Seaman Schepps does this beautifully.*

Why don't you take your old childhood coral beads and have them done up into big pins of flower designs or bracelets, studding the hole…with gold or a tiny diamond? DIANA VREELAND

Coral brooch, c. 1928
Coral beads, diamonds and gold
Diana Vreeland made this star-shaped brooch from a necklace that had been her mother's. Vreeland adored red – it was her trademark colour – and this richly coloured brooch would have looked smart when worn with her other trademark look, Maltese Cross cuffs made by her friend Fulco di Verdura.

I is for India and Interpretation

Of the many foreign destinations the Arpels visited, India was one that held endless appeal over the decades, starting in the 1920s and continuing well into the 1970s. Some visits were about acquisition – the chase for such unique stones as the 'Blue Princess', a sapphire of 114 carats – and some were an artful mix of socializing and selling. But each time, the influence of Indian culture and beauty was carried back to Paris, where new pieces were created based on colours and shapes seen abroad, and with the introduction of under-utilized stones, especially coral.

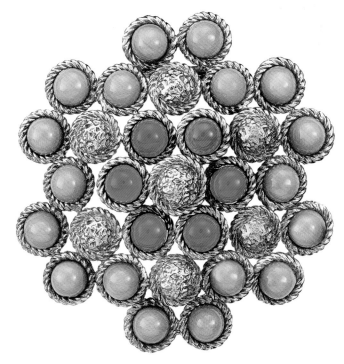

Buddha brooch,
by Van Cleef & Arpels, French, 1927
Platinum, emeralds, rubies,
coral and diamonds
This sumptuous brooch exemplifies the reverence
the French house has for Asian customs
and beliefs as well as customary Asian materials
such as jade and coral. Precious
jewels here stand in for the more traditional
enamels in Asian artworks.

Coral bracelet/necklace,
by Van Cleef & Arpels, French, 1969
Gold, coral and diamonds
This magnificent piece is an interpretation
of jewelry worn by Indian maharajahs.

Cabochon brooch,
by Van Cleef & Arpels, French, 1972
Gold, chrysoprase and coral
A commanding brooch which shows the
influence of Moorish motifs.

Changing Mores, Swinging Jewelry

As the sixties morphed into the seventies, the world as we knew it was gone, and if you were facing in the right direction (politically, the left), then you knew that Dylan, the nasally crooner of the counter-culture, was right, 'the times they are a-changin'. Music was now hip and in your face, art was fun or witty or irreverent (think Andy Warhol, Roy Lichtenstein, Robert Rauschenberg), film stars rubbed shoulders with models and socialites, and fashion did an about-face. What had cinched at the waist now flowed, covered buttons became loops or zippers, hats happily lost their starch and lazily flopped, and hemlines either zoomed thigh-high or cascaded ankle-deep. In jewelry, the taut and trim became freer, more expressive and less exclusive.

First-class precious stones rode coach with semi-precious, enamel was back in business, and hardstones from coral to onyx to jade and chrysoprase stepped into the limelight. For houses such as Bulgari and Van Cleef & Arpels, the emphasis was on wearability, with the sautoir given a facelift. The long chain that had swagged and sagged in the nineteenth century now swung briskly from the necks of the young and the au courant, its angularity less sexy than curves but just as tactile, and as the decade's new form of convertible jewelry the sautoir was always in perfect proportion to the maxi or the mini.

Coral sautoir, by Bulgari, Italian, 1972
Coral, mother-of-pearl, onyx,
diamonds and 18K gold

The four major card suits originated in fifteenth-century France, and of them the spade has long been an etymological mind twister. Although the spade found on English playing cards ultimately derives from the leaf on German cards, its journey there is circuitous, partaking of both French and Italian meanings and word plays. Bulgari adapted the playing card motif on a number of items, including this necklace, which can be shortened and worn as a bracelet.

Coral pendant necklace, by Bulgari,
maker's marks for Pery et Cie,
Italian and French, c. 1975
Coral, onyx, diamonds,
mother-of-pearl and 18K gold

Big. Heavy. Versatile. Wearable. These were
the buzzwords for jewelry in the 1970s, and
Bulgari was one of the houses that moved
with ease away from the more serious jewelry
of the sixties. Even the gold changed: jewelry that
had been made with platinum or white gold
was now ablaze in yellow gold,
a more companionable alloy for the
brighter stones and bolder
colours Bulgari was using.

Coral pendant necklace,
by Bulgari, Italian, 1972
Coral, mother-of-pearl and 18K gold

By the time that Bulgari issued their playing
card pendant necklaces in the early 1970s,
Andy Warhol and Pop Art had proven that
the quotidian could become art. With more than
a whiff of wit, Bulgari took a similar tack: if a
soup can could be the subject of
a painting, why not make a playing
card a piece of fine jewelry?

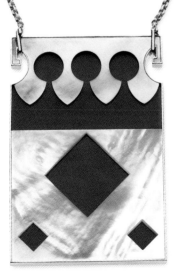

Above left
Playing card brooch, by Bulgari, Italian, c. 1975
Mother-of-pearl, enamel,
diamonds and 18K gold

Within the playing card series created by
Bulgari, this little brooch says it all: the four
playing card symbols, in separate lozenge-
shaped quadrants, each replicate the larger
lozenge inlaid with mother-of-pearl.

**Coral pendant necklace and ear pendants,
by Van Cleef & Arpels, French, 1972**
Coral, green and black onyx and yellow gold
*As though they had taken a dip in the
Fountain of Youth, the coral pendant
necklaces made by Van Cleef & Arpels
from this period were dazzling,
rhythmic and full of life.*

**Coral pendant sautoir,
by Van Cleef & Arpels, New York, c. 1970**
Cabochon coral, green chalcedony, onyx,
diamonds and 18K gold
*The key materials, especially
the coral and onyx, with some sparkle given by
the diamonds, place this among the dynamic
objects made by Van Cleef & Arpels
in the 1970s.*

Coral and black onyx suite,
by Van Cleef & Arpels, French, 1974
Coral, black onyx, diamonds
and yellow gold
*The pendant is removable along with
a bracelet, making this a very versatile set.*

Coral brooch, by Donald Claflin for
Tiffany & Co., American, late 1960s–early 70s
Coral and hydrogrossular garnet beads,
diamonds, platinum and gold
Claflin was an important star in the Tiffany & Co.
crown, and whatever he made – from the serious
to the whimsical (and there was plenty of that)
– had a confidence, a sense of colour and sparkle,
and timely appeal. To understand Claflin is to
understand American jewelry mid-century.

Coral brooch by Donald Claflin for
Tiffany & Co., American, late 1960s–early 70s
Carved coral cherries, diamonds,
platinum and gold
Edible beauty.

Opposite
Four-strand coral bead necklace,
late 20th century
Coral beads, onyx, diamonds
and 18K white gold
A classic Art Deco mingling of coral, onyx
and diamonds, but rendered in the looser look
of the late twentieth century.

A Little Lexicon of Imaginary Beasts

From the heavens to the underworld, from the land to the sea, fabulous creatures abound, some fearsome, others friendly. They may offer warning or salvation, calm the soul or inspire passion, invoke power, cause destruction, or aid in fertility and healing. Whatever their bent, these beasts of myth and religion are part of our collective imagination. Fauns and faeries, satyrs and sea serpents, or beloved unicorns and fabled nymphs appear in art and in literature, in music and in dance, and in objects both ceremonial and decorative. And though artists have always taken liberty with expressing the fabulous, there are a few guidelines as to the what and the who of imaginary beings. In the jeweled kingdom, these are the most common of fabulous beasts:

Chimera—A fire-breathing three-part creature having the head of a lion, the body of a goat and the tail of a dragon. Homer described it similarly, though with the hind parts of a serpent. Considered a representative of evil and ill will. The chimera is the offspring of Typhon and Echidne, and was eventually slain by Bellerophon astride Pegasus.

Dragon—Much has been written about whether dragons are also serpents, and the evidence is compelling on both sides of the debate, but as cast in jewelry they are a breed apart. Dragons are a lot whose origins, traditions and meaning are as ancient and varied as the people who have depicted them: some breathe fire; have wings and fly; are wingless but swim; are perpetual land rovers; live in caves and guard treasure; give life to humans; eat humans; symbolize the dead. Some are kind and giving; others are destructive and exact terrible punishment. Their fiery breath was often reason enough to fear them. Dragons could be all-powerful through their association with the Great Mother, both water god and warrior sun god. According to experts Richard Barber and Anne Riches, dragons had an 'eagle's feet and wings, lion's forelimbs and head, fish's scales, antelope's horns and a serpentine form of trunk and tail, which occasionally extended to the head.' In other words, they were a composite of creatures that flew, walked or swam. On one

Dragon brooch,
by Van Cleef & Arpels,
French, 1969
Gold, emeralds and coral

Griffin brooch,
by Van Cleef & Arpels, French, 1971
Carved pink coral, amethysts, emeralds,
diamonds and gold
'If you don't know what a griffin looks like,
look at the picture,' from Lewis Carroll's
Alice in Wonderland.

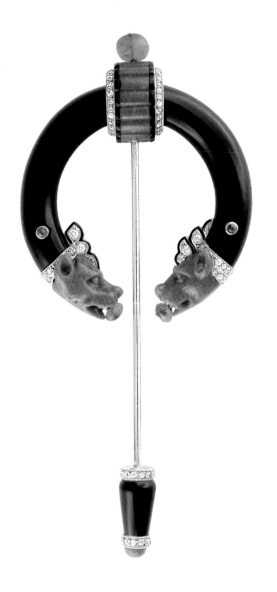

point, however, there is consensus – they were the largest of all beasts. Slaying a dragon was a universal sport, conquered notably by Perseus and St George. The meaning of dragons in myth, including Jung, and in religions worldwide is too vast to list, but in all regards dragons are potent forces. In print, the dragon is ubiquitous, both literally and symbolically, from the Bible to Beowulf, even the Hobbit and Harry Potter.

Griffin, var. gryphon—Most commonly depicted with the head, wings and talons of an eagle and the body and legs of a lion, thus signifying the king of the birds and of the jungle respectively. As a winged creature, it could reach great heights and its enormous wingspan could shield or block the rays of the sun, thus its reputation as a protector of golden treasure, especially in the area to the north of the Hyperboreans. The griffin of India and the Middle East is harmless, whereas its European counterpart is rapacious. Its colouring has been variously described with a degree of exactitude: a deep blue neck, red and black feathers, and white wings. Symbolically, the griffin represents the dual nature of Christ: the divine (eagle) and the human (lion); the Saviour and the Antichrist in Christian art; and, in Egyptian hieroglyphs, heat, based on its association with the sun. The heraldic griffin is shown in profile, with wings and a superbly grand leonine tail, which always seems on the verge of flicking away any less-than-worthy rivals.

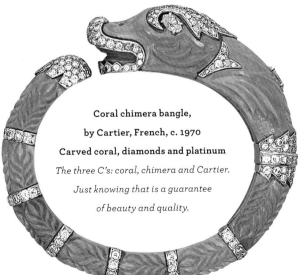

Coral chimera bangle,
by Cartier, French, c. 1970
Carved coral, diamonds and platinum
The three C's: coral, chimera and Cartier.
Just knowing that is a guarantee
of beauty and quality.

Art Deco coral jabot brooch
by Cartier, French?, c. 1925
Carved coral chimera heads, emeralds,
diamonds, onyx and platinum
According to the leading Cartier historian Hans Nadelhoffer,
the Cartier fibula drew its inspiration from a myriad of sources,
including the Far East and seventh-century Merovingian forms.
By 1907, it was already fashionable to close a chic kimono with
a fibula and by the 1920s the Cartier fibula became nearly
synonymous with a brooch. As for the chimera at the terminus,
this beguiling form was bejeweled in a number of ways by Cartier
and became a leading motif for the house.

Dragon bracelet,

by Van Cleef & Arpels, French, 1974

Gold, coral, sapphires, emeralds and diamonds

As the signs always say in the zoo,

'Please don't pet the animals'.

**Coral elephant bangle,
by David Webb, American, c. 1970s?
Carved coral, diamonds, cabochon sapphire
and emeralds, platinum and 18K gold**

*Webb specialized in a cunning mix of the
social and the professional, and when he made
fashion statements, as he was wont to do, the
cream of society – from New York to Palm Beach
to Houston – listened. Among his bons mots:
'Casual rich is the look today. If you have a
40-carat diamond, it has to be shoved into gold.
It has to be doing something. Everything has
to be young and fun.' 'Today a piece of jewelry
shouldn't look valuable. The trend is similar
to the twenties and thirties when people didn't
want to look rich and Chanel piled on beads and
pearls with her simplest things. It's a played
down, low-key look as opposed to the
diamond thing.'*

**Coral dragon bangle, by Cartier, French, 1947
Carved coral dragon heads, cabochon
emeralds, diamonds and 18K gold**

*This Cartier bangle was among the treasures
owned by the Duchess of Windsor, whose
provenance power is hard to overstate: her
jewelry, her clothes, her home furnishings,
even the type of dogs that roamed the Windsor
residences influenced popular taste.*

> *Coral has a whole new pizzazz about it. It's timely, gay, young, it's not precious and it's a becoming colour with the pale lipsticks.* DAVID WEBB

David Webb, Fun but Never Frivolous

Jacqueline Kennedy Onassis called him a modern-day Cellini, whereas the Duchess of Windsor thought he followed in the hushed footsteps of Fabergé. Regardless of his presumed historical pedigree, Webb was a man of his time, both artist and trendsetter. He wanted to make the very best jewelry possible and he wanted to see his pieces worn with exuberance and style. His roots were in the American South (he was born a few years ahead of the Depression in Asheville, North Carolina), but Webb's sensibility was decidedly urban and urbane. By the time he was twenty-three, David Webb had opened his first shop in New York, eventually claiming 7 East 57th Street – among the most coveted addresses in retail – as his personal commercial atelier. For Webb, the 1960s offered an opportunity to affect a change in how women accessorized. In the pre-revolutionary 1960s, his big jewelry was intended to offset demure dresses offered up as fashion aperitifs by Oleg Cassini, but by the end of the decade change was everywhere, and Webb's emancipated woman, her hair now long and wild or sharply Sassooned, was boldly wearing Mary Quant and Courrèges, or the architectural creations of modernist Geoffrey Beene. This 'new woman' was unapologetic in her outlook and lifestyle, further asserted with Webb's chunky necklaces and expressive bracelets. Wearing Webb meant you were a member of the sixties' newest (anti-)establishment: young, fun and alive.

But fun did not mean frivolous to Webb. The man who designed the Freedom Medal for President Kennedy also took his role as Webb the Tastemaker seriously: 'I stay up nights worrying what I will do next.'

Coral Maltese Cross brooch,
by David Webb, American, c. 1970s
Cabochon coral, cabochon sapphire, diamonds,
enamel and 18K gold
Although the Maltese Cross is a longstanding and potent religious symbol, the adaptation of this Byzantine form into popular jewelry is only in the past two hundred years or so: in the mid-nineteenth century it appears in tortoiseshell, jet and Vauxhall glass, and a century later is first interpreted as a cuff by Verdura for Chanel, who then creates her own version, as does David Webb, seen here.

Carved coral lion bangle,
by David Webb, American, c. 1970s
Coral, diamonds, emeralds,
platinum and 18K gold
By the time David Webb received a Coty, the coveted American fashion award, in 1964, he had released the animal bracelets that have since become the defining icons of his style. Some were coated with enamel, many were carved from coral and studded with emeralds or diamonds, such as this fabulous bangle owned by Elizabeth Taylor. These were jungle beasts designed to walk the city streets – elephants, tigers, dragons and mythical chimeras became Webb Everlasting, glories of his craftsmanship and imagination.

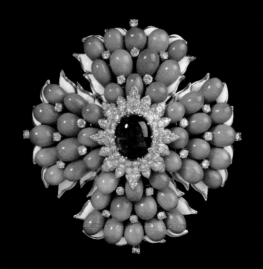

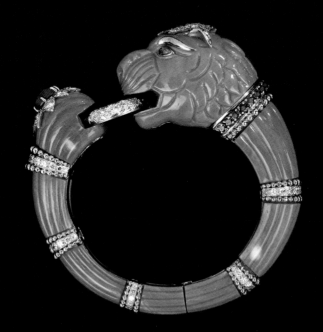

Coral pendant,
American, c. 1950s
Coral, diamonds, cabochon turquoise,
platinum and 18K gold
This sumptuously designed
brooch is made from one piece
of coral. The ribbon of diamonds and gold
that encircle the fluted coral end in
a sweet flourish, almost like an afterthought
– a casually tied bow of gold braid.

Coral Machine Age ear clips,

c. 1930?

Coral beads and gold

Machine Age meets the modern age.

Oval-link bracelet, by Pomellato,
Italian, c. late 1960s-early 1970s
Coral cabochons and 18K gold

Pino Rabolini founded Pomellato in Milan in
1967, and introduced the idea of prêt-à-porter
jewelry. That was forty years ago, and the jewelry
continues to showcase beautiful stones, often
cabochon cut, with easy to wear, stylish settings.

Coral necklace and bracelet,
by William Spratling,
American/Mexican, c. 1947
Cabochon coral and 18K gold

Although he's best known for his work in silver
and wood, this coral and gold group shows
Spratling's reverence for his materials: the coral
beads are rendered simply but nobly.

Ballet and Van Cleef & Arpels: A Perfect Duet

Ballet is mother's milk to Van Cleef & Arpels. This was especially so for Louis Arpels, son of the company's founder, and for Louis's nephew, Claude, whom he took to the Paris engagement of Diaghilev's Ballets Russes in May of 1921. That season they saw Michel Fokine's spectacular ballet *The Firebird*, with music by Igor Stravinsky. A few years later, they would see the original production of *Apollon Musagète*, again with music by Stravinsky, but also unveiling the brilliant choreography of the little known George Balanchine. By 1939, Van Cleef & Arpels had opened a shop in New York City, with key members of the Arpels family in position, including Louis and Claude. Their passion for dance had only increased, and in 1940 Van Cleef & Arpels launched an inaugural collection of jewelry inspired by dance. It was to be the first of many homages to the beauty of ballet. On the Van Cleef stage, *petite mignonne* ballerinas fashioned as brooches are resplendent in diamonds – on their arms and skirts, their faces typically a sweetheart rose-cut diamond, their diamond toe shoes refracting light everywhere. But it is the other precious stones – the emeralds, rubies and sapphires – that give decoration to a skirt, sparkle to a tiara, colour to a bouquet of flowers. These are ballerinas in arabesque, en pointe, performing sous-sus and relevé. In 1950, Van Cleef & Arpels designed a collier of ballerinas in diamonds and yellow gold that was to be a motif for decades to come. By 1961, a relationship had been established between Van Cleef & Arpels and George Balanchine, but that's another chapter in the esteemed jeweler's enduring relationship with ballet.

Opposite

**'Ballerina' coral necklace
and ear clips, by Van Cleef & Arpels,
French, 1997
Carved coral, diamonds and 18K gold**

*Of the many collections introduced by Van Cleef
& Arpels, the ballerina has a history with the
house that dates to 1940 and reflects the passion
of at least two members of the Arpels family,
Louis and Claude. This necklace, resplendent
in three hues of coral, has precedent
in an earlier model from 1950. The dancer in
the centre, shown in both white and deep coral,
is en pointe with her left foot sur le cou-de-pied
derrière, surrounded on either side by dancers
in third arabesque carved in medium coral.*

**'Rose de Noël' coral suite,
by Van Cleef & Arpels, French, 1995
Coral, green chalcedony,
diamonds and 18K gold**

*Van Cleef & Arpels introduced the
'Rose de Noel' pattern in the 1970s.
Around this time gold was costly, so Claude
Arpels turned to other materials such as
coral and wood, and in this instance he made
spectacular use of coral. The scale is grand
(at its widest, the necklace is 5 inches [12.7 cm]
across), the impression of the roses is iconic,
and even the alternating hues of the red and
pink coral, interspersed with green chalcedony,
have a formality that bespeaks the highest
of jewelry fashion.*

Coral necklace, by de Grisogono, Swiss, 2007
Angel skin coral, brown diamonds,
and 18K rose gold

Try to imagine twenty-four lozenges of icy pink
coral against your skin – how lucky you would be
to have the experience of wearing this one-of-
a-kind necklace. This Geneva-based jewelry
company has only been in business since 1993,
yet its founder and owner, Fawaz Gruosi, has
already established de Grisogono as a serious
house, excelling in jeweled watches, black
diamonds and extremely rich design.

Coral brooch and ear pendants,
Italian?, c. 19th century
Carved angel skin coral leaves
and carved tortoiseshell flies

The palest coral – angel skin – with the rich
honey tones of tortoiseshell: this is nature
sublimely realized. The insects are so realistic
that one expects them to move or fly about,
which speaks to the accomplishment of the
artist who carved this piece.

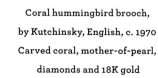

Coral hummingbird brooch,
by Kutchinsky, English, c. 1970
Carved coral, mother-of-pearl,
diamonds and 18K gold

In the nineteenth century, it was remarked that
the hummingbird 'is a jeweler's bird', which is
quite true given its diminutive size, its needle-
thin beak, and of course the brilliancy of its
colourful plumage. Kutchinsky conveys the
bird's characteristic mid-air hover.

Carved coral parrot,
by Cartier, French?, late 1940s
Coral, diamonds, onyx, emeralds,
platinum and 18K gold

The parrot is wildly coloured – especially those
in tropical rainforests – though this all-orange
version is more a figment of the jeweler's
imagination than of anything found in nature.

Coral bird brooch,
by Cartier, French?, c. 1950
Carved coral, diamonds, cabochon sapphire,
cultured pearl, platinum and 18K gold

These bejeweled birds are perched upon an
exquisitely carved coral mound, depicting a
massing of peonies, chrysanthemums, daffodils
and dahlias.

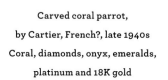

Coral sea urchin dress clips,
by Tiffany & Co., American, c. 1960s
Carved coral and 18K gold

There was a time when the well-attired woman wore dress clips. She'd pin them to her dress or cardigan (imagine how these Tiffany clips would light up a black sheath or a winter white cashmere cardigan), clip them to a neck ribbon, to matching suit pockets, use them to jazz up a beret, or to swag or cinch the strap on her evening gown. Their heyday was circa 1930 through the 1950s, though some were worn into the early 1960s. This coral pair by Tiffany is remarkable for its rarity, and with the Tiffany sea urchin brooch, seen below, would form a suite of great style.

Coral rings, by Monica Rossi, Italian, c. 2005
Carved coral crab and octopus and 18K gold

The simplest way to imagine either ring is that your hand is a beach and that this large coral crab or octopus has taken to nesting there. These unusual rings are by the Milanese jeweler Monica Rossi, who goes by the professional name Anaconda.

Coral sea urchin brooch,
by Tiffany & Co., American, c. 1960s
Carved coral and 18K gold

A classic, and one that is uniquely a Tiffany creation.

A Starfish By Any Other Name is a Sea Star (Asterias forbesii)

Scientists like to begin a discussion of starfish with the opening gambit that the term itself is all wrong. Incorrect, inaccurate, and frankly no longer acceptable – except to the general public who are attached to its longstanding name. The problem? Starfish aren't fish and hence should more properly be called sea stars. Fish, for example, use gills to breathe and a tail to help propel them in water. The sea star / starfish uses its tube feet to motor along – they even breathe through these feet as well through tiny breathing tubes all over their bodies. And whereas fish have eyes, the best the sea star has in that department is a purple eyespot on each arm to detect light and dark. The campaign for a name change makes sense.

As to the rugged little fighter, the sea star is an echinoderm, meaning 'spiny skin', which gives it built-in armour against such predators as crabs. It's a climber, too, over rocks or ledges, which it also uses as a defensive ploy. As an echinoderm, the sea star's cousins include sea urchins and sand dollars. Nor is the sea star fussy about real estate, making its home in all the world's oceans, from warm tropical waters to the bitterly cold polar regions. Above all, what the sea star has in spades is arms (some have as many as twenty or forty) and more colours and patterns than most women have in their closets. Perhaps its colourful outerwear is what has made it so long appealing to jewelry designers, and the fact that a star – whether in the heavens or the sea – is one of nature's most perfect forms.

'Coral star' brooch, by Schlumberger
for Tiffany & Co.,
French, 1956
Coral, platinum, gold and diamonds
*For a number of his delightful creations,
Schlumberger found inspiration in the sea.
But leave it to the artful Frenchman to imbue
the often-used motif of the starfish with such
invention: the energetic coral cones are like
bursts of fireworks, reaching in every direction.*

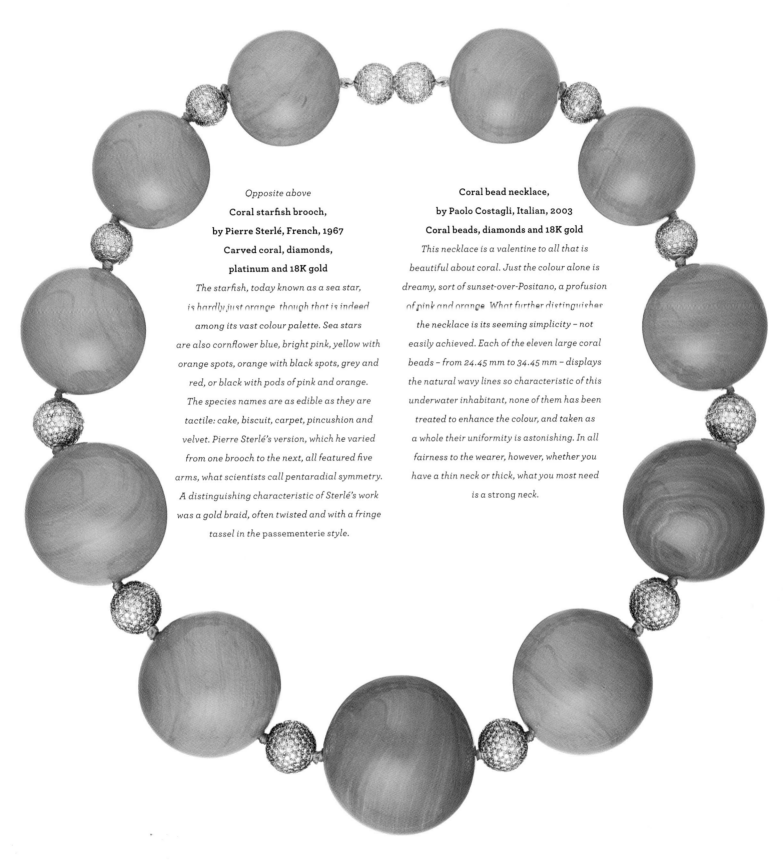

Opposite above

Coral starfish brooch,

by Pierre Sterlé, French, 1967

Carved coral, diamonds,

platinum and 18K gold

The starfish, today known as a sea star,
is hardly just orange, though that is indeed
among its vast colour palette. Sea stars
are also cornflower blue, bright pink, yellow with
orange spots, orange with black spots, grey and
red, or black with pods of pink and orange.
The species names are as edible as they are
tactile: cake, biscuit, carpet, pincushion and
velvet. Pierre Sterlé's version, which he varied
from one brooch to the next, all featured five
arms, what scientists call pentaradial symmetry.
A distinguishing characteristic of Sterlé's work
was a gold braid, often twisted and with a fringe
tassel in the passementerie style.

Coral bead necklace,

by Paolo Costagli, Italian, 2003

Coral beads, diamonds and 18K gold

This necklace is a valentine to all that is
beautiful about coral. Just the colour alone is
dreamy, sort of sunset-over-Positano, a profusion
of pink and orange. What further distinguishes
the necklace is its seeming simplicity – not
easily achieved. Each of the eleven large coral
beads – from 24.45 mm to 34.45 mm – displays
the natural wavy lines so characteristic of this
underwater inhabitant, none of them has been
treated to enhance the colour, and taken as
a whole their uniformity is astonishing. In all
fairness to the wearer, however, whether you
have a thin neck or thick, what you most need
is a strong neck.

**'Forbidden City' necklace,
by Jean Vendome, French, 1997
Coral and branch coral, nephrite, old jade,
garnets and yellow gold**

*Jean Vendome is an enthusiast of natural
materials – branch coral, fossil ammonites,
crab claws – combined in surprising ways
with crystals, agate or pearls. This particular
necklace was specifically commissioned to
feature materials native to Asia.*

**'Valparaiso Idyll' bracelet, by Victoire de
Castellane for Dior, French, 2009
Coral, mother-of-pearl, diamonds, white
opal, fire opal, chalcedony, cultured baroque
pearls, red and pink spinels, pink, purple,
and orange sapphires, tsavorite garnets,
18K rose gold and lacquer**

*When Victoire de Castellane launched the Dior
fine jewelry collection in 1998, she stamped
it with her own canny style and whimsy. This
colourful bracelet (the seahorse and flowers can*

*be worn separately, either as pendants or
as brooches) is part of a collection known as
Idyllic Paradises, which includes 'Fiji', 'Borneo',
'Kyoto Gardens' and 'Valparaiso', in Chile,
once called the Jewel of the Pacific. De
Castellane is herself a rare jewel of sorts, as the
descendant of a family that dates to the 10th
century. The sense of legacy – hers and Dior's
– seems a natural fit, updated by constant
creativity. As de Castellane says, 'I wish
I could have my brain scanned.'*

3.

Horn,
The Queen of Art Nouveau

*J*ust as monkfish is sometimes called the poor man's lobster, horn has been on more than one occasion referred to as 'mockshell', an inferior imitation of tortoiseshell in the eyes of late-nineteenth and early-twentieth-century connoisseurs. Among those still becoming accustomed to the swift changes brought about by Art Nouveau (goodbye diamonds, hello moonstones and coloured glass), horn was dismissed as common, ordinary, the scullery maid of the new materials being turned into jewelry. But just as in the Cinderella tale, once cleaned up and dressed up with pearls or such semi-precious stones as opal, horn could measure up to the finest ivory and tortoiseshell Art Nouveau jewelry.

It was a question of being at the right place at the right time: by the mid-1890s, women had grown fatigued with the weight of history adorning their bodices and hanging from their ears, the various revivalist movements by this time seeming dusty, fussy, overdone and overworked. Clothing too was changing, with lighter fabrics in vogue requiring jewelry that neither pulled nor damaged the soft silks and organzas. Japonisme had reached the shores of Europe and was affecting in its brilliant use of asymmetry and its emphasis on natural forms and less precious materials. Whereas the Aesthetic movement depicted shorebirds or insects and butterflies in exacting detail, Art Nouveau imbued them with flair, imagination and interpretation. A lazy dragonfly of yore morphed into a fantasy figure commanding power and allegiance, and exuding unabashed sensuality. Indeed, the female nude and femininity were hallmarks of Art Nouveau, as was an emphasis on beauty or inherent versus material value. Horn was at this crossroads of change, there for the taking, an easy, malleable and inexpensive medium for expressing the jewelry being made by such masters as René Lalique, Henri Vever and Paul Liénard. Lalique, in fact, has the distinction of being the first artist to show horn jewelry, which he introduced in 1896 at the Salon of the Société des Artistes Français.

Art Nouveau horn tiara, by René Lalique, French, c. 1900

The story of horn, then, is inextricably a part of Art Nouveau, which was short-lived – a mere fifteen years or so, from about 1895 to 1910 – but influential, an important turning point in the world of decorative arts. Part of horn's success was in fact its affordability in comparison to the growing costliness of tortoiseshell and ivory, plus its availability. Whereas tortoiseshell was derived mainly from the scutes of the hawksbill turtle, any number of mammals could provide horn, among them oxen, water buffalo, rams, goats, and the American buffalo, thereby opening up a larger supply of this common material from Europe, Southeast Asia and the United States.

Horn has a creaminess that ranges from near white to charcoal black, a palette largely due to the pigment melanin, the same substance that in humans determines eye, hair and skin colour (and makes us tan). Like tortoiseshell, horn is a thermoplastic that when heated can be moulded and pulled into a variety of forms, making it a receptive medium for inlaying stones or plique-à-jour enamelling, one of the signature techniques of Art Nouveau. Prior to this time, horn had been used to make such functional objects as bowls or serving spoons (it is both waterproof and greaseless), the tips of canes and assorted walking sticks, even buttons. But it was Lalique and his contemporaries who looked to domestic cattle horn for this new jewelry and manipulated it in fresh ways, through bleaching or dying, thus rendering it anything but commonplace.

Diadems and tiaras, neck plaques, hair combs and statement-making necklaces were formed with the sheerest horn adorned with pearls, pavé diamonds, gold, semi-precious stones and enamelling. A perfect example of horn's ascendance and diamond's transition as an accent is Lalique's diadem depicting fern leaves, page 66. Nature has been transformed – not demoted or marginalized, but shown to be more fragile, more feminine, evocative rather than explicative. Henri Vever, *the* chronicler of nineteenth-century French jewelry, is similarly inclined, and in his horn and pearl sycamore hairpin of 1900 there is both a simplicity and delicacy altogether fresh.

All of this had changed by the time the twentieth century was steaming toward a close, with horn now being shown off more prominently – again artisanal, again fashionable, but shown off differently. Now it is lacquered by Hermès, or mixed with such materials as wood, mother-of-pearl and faux stones by fashion houses, or allowed to be its simplest self, in a pair of earrings by Gabriella Kiss. The artist calls them clipper ships, and with their diminutive horn sails and sapphire briolettes signifying water, horn in its many uses continues to appeal to artists and designers, a sign that perhaps now, at the end of the first decade of the twenty-first century, horn is having a mini revival.

Previous page
Art Nouveau horn tiara,
by René Lalique,
French, c. 1900
Horn, pearls, enamel and gold
Lalique takes the form of a traditional tiara, but instead of studding it with the sparkle of diamonds, he looks to a material that is more in keeping with spirit of the 'New Art' of late nineteenth-, early twentieth-century France. Horn is used here to suggest the leaves of a hazelnut tree interspersed with pearl blossoms.

Opposite left
Art Nouveau horn apple blossom
wreath by Paul Liénard, French, c. 1900
Horn, pearls, diamonds and gold
Liénard may be less well-known among Art Nouveau artists, yet there is nothing second-rate about this wreath. The delicate handling of the horn and the gentle floral trails show that Liénard was in full command of his materials. Innocence, youth, beauty, purity – each is conveyed in these delicate spring blossoms.

Opposite right
Art Nouveau horn sycamore leaf hair comb,
by Henri Vever, French, c. 1900
Horn, pearls and gold
It may be small, but Vever's sycamore comb is a tour de force of the imagination. Superficially, the sycamore flower does not appear feminine, though in fact Vever depicts it at its most potent: when the seed is fertilized, it forms a wing-like shape, what botanists call a double samara, which resembles the blades of a helicopter when carried airborne by the wind.

M. Lalique is courageously Parisian in the way that he gives his great imaginative skill to the splendours of fashion. INTERNATIONAL STUDIO, 1905

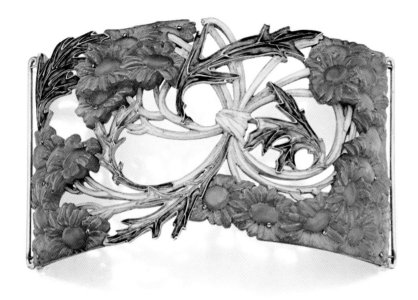

**Art Nouveau horn chrysanthemum
dog collar plaque, by René Lalique,
French, c. 1900**
Horn, enamel and gold
*The chrysanthemum was one of the classic
flowers depicted in Art Nouveau, influenced
by Japonisme that was appearing in parts of
Western Europe, especially France and Britain.*

**Art Nouveau horn fern leaf diadem,
by René Lalique, French, c. 1905**
Horn, diamonds and gold
*Ferns are older than dinosaurs and land
animals, and with a history going back 360
million years, they are in fact the first land plant,
although they aren't exotic like the orchid, so
beloved by artists of the Art Nouveau. However,
the non-flowering fern has an unusual life cycle,
and perhaps this appealed to Lalique. Here the
ferns are gently massed, shown to luminous
effect by thin sheets of horn with their fragile,
diamond-covered stems.*

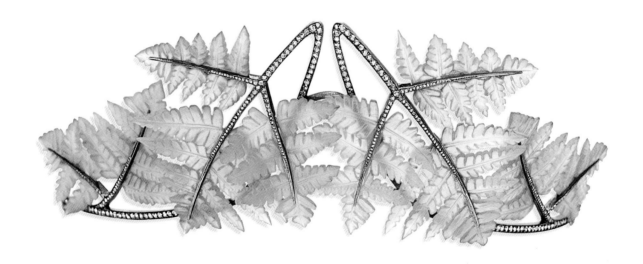

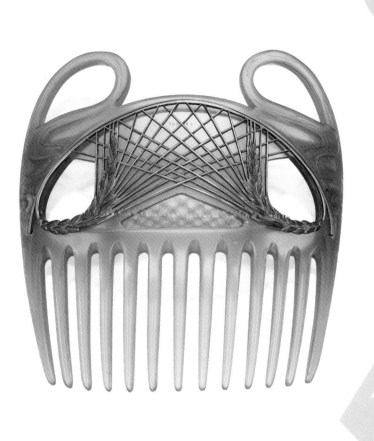

Art Nouveau horn hair comb,
by René Lalique, French, c. 1900
Horn, enamel and gold
The comb is not even 5 inches (13 cm) wide,
yet there is fine detail throughout, from the
signature Art Nouveau whiplash scrolls
bordering the gold plaque, designed in the form
of wheat stalks, to the applied enamel adding
to the realistic decoration.

**Art Nouveau horn intertwined
serpents brooch, by René Lalique,
French, c. 1902**

Carved horn, pearls, glass and gold

*Though the Victorians seemed to produce
a hefty amount of jewelry featuring snakes
(Queen Victoria's engagement ring was a snake
with its tail in its mouth, a symbol of eternity),
the artists of the Art Nouveau also drew on this
most ancient of motifs. As Nicolas Boileau-
Despréaux, a seventeenth-century French poet
wrote, 'There is no snake, no odious monster,
that imitated by art, cannot charm one's eyes.'*

**Antelope bracelet,
by Van Cleef & Arpels, French, 1974**

Gold and buffalo horn

*Although this bracelet is actually made with
buffalo horn, its depiction of an antelope
bespeaks the surprisingly varied horns of the
antelope: they may be curved and face front or
back, twisted, lyrate (in the shape of a lyre),
or even recurved. One further point: unlike
antlers, the horns of these high-loping
creatures are not made of bone.*

The Roar of René Lalique at the St Louis World's Fair

This massive necklace made its debut far away from Paris, at the Louisiana Purchase Exposition of 1904 held in St Louis, Missouri. (Ironically, this marked the centenary of the 1803 Louisiana Purchase by the United States of formerly French-owned territory.) It was at the St Louis World's Fair, as the exposition was informally better known, among exhibits from forty-three of the forty-five states and sixty-two foreign countries that Henry Walters made the purchase of this necklace. Walters, the scion of a successful railroad businessman from Baltimore, was also the heir to a vast and important collection begun by his father, and had recently taken a seat on the board of the Metropolitan Museum of Art in New York. By 1909 Walters would open his family's personal art gallery to the public, and not long after his death in 1931 the gallery would become the foundation of the esteemed Walters Museum in Baltimore.

**Art Nouveau horn tiger necklace,
by René Lalique, French, c. 1903**
Horn, tortoiseshell, enamel, agate and gold
*Lalique made this necklace – which actually
looks more ceremonial than fashionable
– nearly a decade after gallerist Siegfried Bing
introduced the notion of an 'Art Nouveau'.
Lalique's confidence, his bold and unorthodox*
*use of formerly utilitarian materials, and his
mastery of form and figure come together in this
spectacular necklace. Everything about it is
feline, from the tigers restlessly circling the gold
collar – the horn is ideally suited to showing
off their musculature – to the agate mounts
that end in a curve, suggesting claws, and
the tortoiseshell incisors.*

Hermès and Horn: A Story of Tradition, Beauty and Anatomy

In some contexts the word *tradition* implies something airless, stuffy, stubbornly mired in the past. But when the same word is applied to Hermès, it is triumphant, it sings, much the way it sounds when pronounced in French, with a bit of a lilt to the last syllable. For more than six generations, this family-owned company has steadfastly dedicated itself to tradition and the pursuit of perfection, working with artisans worldwide in their unwavering quest. For the creation of their horn and lacquer jewelry, Hermès went to Ho Chi Minh City in Vietnam, where family ateliers excel at working with buffalo horn. There horn and lacquer jewelry – hair pins, cuffs, pendants and sautoirs – is made with tremendous care and classic style.

There is nothing quick about this process, but then again Hermès has never as a company been ruled by the clock or the balance sheet. Once the horn is chosen, the process of perfecting it begins: trimming, drying, applying oils, compressing, cutting, piercing, hollowing, scraping, buffing, polishing. From there, part two of the creation begins, with the application of lacquer, a natural vegetable resin, and once more the process is precise, delineated, deliberate. As the company says, 'Craftsmanship is not a struggle. It is a quest.'

Horn sautoir and cuff,
by Hermès, French, c. 2007
Horn and lacquered horn
When it comes to the finest in classic design,
the name Hermès is at the top of any list
worldwide, and today that name is discreetly
expressed by the letter 'H', as in
this two-tone cuff.

I approach making jewelry as though it's small sculpture.

GABRIELLA KISS

**Horn clipper ship ear pendants,
by Gabriella Kiss, American, 2004
Horn, briolette sapphires, and 18K gold**
*Buffalo horn has a natural curve, making it
especially suitable for suggesting the billowing
sails of a clipper ship, a heavily rigged, fast-
gliding boat dating from the nineteenth century.*

4.

Ivory,
The Cream of the
Jeweler's Canvas

I

Ivory bangle and ear clips, by Buccellati, Italian, c. 1945

*S*ay the word ivory and sophistication comes to mind – ivory card stock is always sublime for letter writing; an ivory cashmere sweater is the ne plus ultra of cool-weather stylishness; the ideal vanilla ice cream looks ivory and tastes slightly exotic. It's the way that something done in ivory tips the scales just so that puts it in a category both refined and, yes, exotic. Which makes sense, for when it comes to jewelry the ivory most often used came from one of the largest mammals of the African savannah, the African elephant, *Loxodonta Africana*.

The animal's heavy tusks proved irresistible to hunters and so it was that the African elephant and its smaller cousin, the Asian elephant, *Elephas maximus*, became the source for choice ivory, well into the latter half of the twentieth century. Both the superior colour and density of African ivory prevailed over Asian ivory for carving, although much beautiful work with Asian ivory has historically been made in India and parts of Japan and China. Tusks or teeth from other beasts have also been used for ivory goods, chiefly the American sperm whale, *Physeter macrocephalus*, and to a lesser degree the orca, *Orcinus orca* (technically a dolphin, though better known by the misnomer 'killer whale'), both of which were used for New England whalers' traditional scrimshaw work.

Ivory carving is a centuries-old art, and by the waning years of the 1800s ivory jewelry was being produced in quantity in France, Belgium, and, to a lesser degree, in Britain. In Brussels, where ivory had arrived from the Belgian Congo, goldsmith Philippe Wolfers set to work, influenced in large part by the Japanese decorative arts and the burgeoning style of the Art Nouveau. By 1897 his work had gained renown, but three years later across the border the real fireworks were going off at the famous Exposition Universelle of 1900, in Paris. It was here, in the 'City of Light', that Art Nouveau artists such as René Lalique and Henri Vever claimed both this new style and material for showing a new kind of beauty – natural and exquisite, luxurious but simple. Consider, for example, an

It was a quiet way – / He asked if I was his – / I made no answer of the Tongue / But answer of the Eyes…

EMILY DICKINSON, c. 1865

orchid comb made by Lalique around 1903: his stunning workmanship in ivory makes his cattleya orchid an exemplar of verisimilitude, an Orchid Everlasting. Sensuality and sinuous form describe Lalique's female nude brooch of circa 1900, her seductive beauty owing to the facile medium and richness of ivory. Forty years later, the great Verdura, Sicilian by birth but Paris-based by choice and eventually a resident of New York, used ivory to acclaim in various figural objects, including his magical unicorns adorned with rubies, sapphires and emeralds, or his ivory Indian chessman of 1940, turbaned, astride horses, with pet lemurs and leopards. By mid-century, Tiffany, Schlumberger and Seaman Schepps also were making figural pieces (Schlumberger's flower brooch is a notch more stylized than Lalique's orchid) in contrast to dressy ivory bangles by the likes of Buccellati and David Webb, embedded with cabochon gemstones, or with gem-set stones by Van Cleef & Arpels.

In the 1970s, as conservation efforts to protect elephants gained momentum, jewelers found a surprisingly abundant source for ivory: mammoths, extinct for millions of years and yet, like amber, preserved in time, in this case thanks to deep freezing. The habitat of this prehistoric beast, known as the woolly or tundra mammoth, began in Africa and spread to Europe, Siberia, and eventually North America. Its significance for jewelers today is that they can use its pre-served ivory with a clear conscience and free hand.

Contemporary work includes that of the ultra modernist Ted Muehling, whose ivory cuff with its large facets is all sleek flat plains in contrast to the whimsy of Jessica Kagan Cushman, who revives the American whaler's art of scrimshaw with plucky sayings engraved on ivory bangles. Sophistication and gravitas merge in the atelier of Patricia Von Musulin, whose all-ivory necklaces, cuffs and earrings, or those combined with ebony, prove the point that ivory is always elegant, any hour of the day.

Previous page
Ivory bangle and ear clips,
by Buccellati, Italian, c. 1945
Carved ivory flowerheads, sapphires
and 18K gold
Even without the signature, jewelry
by Buccellati declares itself. Mario Buccellati,
who gave the Italian firm his name, was a master
goldsmith with an innate understanding of
embroidery and weaving, for everywhere in the
Buccellati line there are pieces that look
like silk or lace or brocade. The eye for
detail and recall of Renaissance techniques,
as in the carved ivory flowers and sapphires
that rim this bangle, are among the telling
features of Buccellati jewelry.

Ivory bird pendant brooch
with gold neck wire, French, c. 1970s
Ivory and 18K gold
The large scale of this pendant is in keeping
with the 1970s, when jewelry was as 'big and
swinging' as the times.

Secret Tokens of Love

Why an eye? The courting Georgian could gain a measure of secrecy from the prying eyes of society by offering a hard-to-recognize token of him- or herself through the artful rendering of just one eye, typically painted on ivory. This 'lover's eye' jewelry, as it came to be known, was made up as a brooch, a ring or – most discreet of all – a locket.

Ivory eye brooch,
c. early 19th century
Ivory, seed pearls, watercolour
paints and gold

Ivory eye pendant,
c. early 19th century
Ivory, seed pearls, watercolour
paints and gold

Tinted ivory flower brooch,

English, c. 1860

Tinted carved ivory and gold

The flower is Camellia japonica 'pink perfection',
though it was known as Usu-otome in its native
Asia. By 1775, Carl Linnaeus, the Swedish
botanist and father of modern taxonomy,
had named the fragrant genus Camellia in
posthumous honour of George Joseph Kamel,
a Jesuit missionary and pioneering botanist
(who later Latinized his name to Camellus).

There are about two hundred species of
camellias, some of which live four hundred years,
which is happy news for those blessed with this
plant whose blossoms are so abundant that it is
described as a 'formal double'.

Ivory brooch by Cartier, c. 1955

Carved ivory hand, diamonds and 18K gold

This simple little hand, pretty and quite feminine
with its lace ruff, signified friendship and love,
and was made during the early years of Queen
Victoria's reign. It was also produced in
coral and jet.

Orchids, A Temperamental Beauty

Well before the charged flower paintings by the American artist Georgia O'Keeffe, the artists of the Art Nouveau were creating depictions of flowers that steamed with suggestion and eroticism. The orchid, both exotic and rare, and from such faraway places as South America, held centre stage in nineteenth-century England, not unlike the tulipmania of the Dutch Golden Age. The orchid that Lalique carved from ivory and horn was the newly named *Cattleya*, in honour of William Cattley of Barnet, England, a collector of ferns and other tropicals. But the cattleya was not the first orchid imported onto English soil, so why single it out? For one thing, it was exquisitely coloured, and had a large lip, or labellum, unique at the time. John Lindley, the young botanist who named the plant *Cattleya labiata* in 1821 after Cattley, wrote: 'There is certainly no plant of which I have any knowledge that can be said to stand forth with an equal radiance of splendour and beauty.' This kind of showy beauty was the reward of great skill and effort, however, and over the years as more species were discovered and later cultivated in England, the large-flowered cattleyas remained the pinnacle of a plantsman's skills, available mainly to the landed gentry. The 'rich man's plant', as it was nicknamed, became the pursuit of wealthy amateurs and further burnished the plant's exotic appeal. By the early 1890s more than 25,000 *C. labiata* were imported annually into England alone, and the mania for this temperamental beauty had also spread to the Continent and America. When Lalique turned nature into something new, the cattleyas were the flower of choice, fertile enough for this Frenchman's unbound imagination.

**Art Nouveau ivory orchid hair comb,
by René Lalique, French, c. 1903–4
Ivory, horn, plique-à-jour enamel,
diamonds and 18K gold**

*Everything about this comb is extraordinary:
it was made by the greatest of the Art Nouveau
artists; depicts the cattleya, known as the 'Queen
of Orchids'; and is carved from a single piece of
ivory. The three leaves are rendered in plique-à-
jour enamel, from a pale peach to a light olive,
with the veining in light grey enamel studded
with a row of graduated diamonds. The orchid
stem is attached by a gold hinge
to a three-pronged hair comb.*

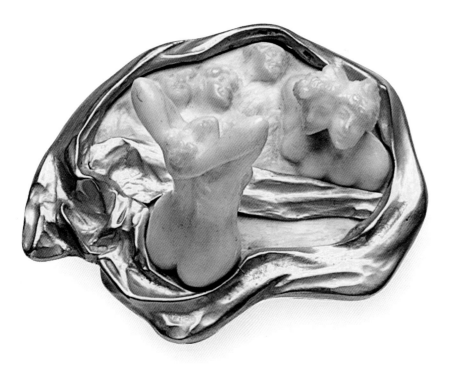

Ivory and the Fin-de-Siècle Woman

More than any other major art movement, Art Nouveau celebrated women – and in ivory the female figure could be shown at her fullest, most expressive best. By the turn of the twentieth century, along with emancipation from tight corsets and repressed sexuality (Sigmund Freud had recently published his now-famous *Interpretation of Dreams* and introduced the term 'psychoanalysis'), women were gaining greater independence. Whereas the woman of the Victorian age would have been scandalized to wear anything suggestive of female nudity in public, the *fin-de-siècle* woman met the Art Nouveau bejeweled nude and embraced her. It was a matter of perfect timing and perfect pitch – women who had rejected mass- or machine-made jewelry in the waning years of the 1800s wanted to wear the new artistic jewelry, *la bijouterie*; nature, liberation

and imagination were the unofficial buzzwords of the Art Nouveau movement, and ivory was the ideal medium for showing the human form in all its luscious sexuality and strength.

Lalique recognized this and carved expressive sculptures of the female in ivory: a brooch of a group of bathers, the figures achingly real and sensual; the kiss brooch of circa 1900–2, two lovers in an endless embrace, the Eros of the piece intensified by the smooth, creamy ivory; the Phryne Cameo Brooch of 1900–2, depicting the celebrated beauty of ancient Greece. Yet it is in the heavenly Belle de Nuit brooch, of circa 1900, attributed to Edmond Becker, that the idealized woman soars with greatness. It is a triumph of female beauty and grace, ideally shown in ivory.

Plique-à-jour, A Celebration of Light and Colour

How fitting that so brilliant a technique as plique-à-jour had its roots in the colourful goldsmith, engraver, artist, writer, musician and all-around Lothario, Benvenuto Cellini. This was in the late 1500s, though its greatest historical impact was among Art Nouveau artists, some three hundred years later. At its most reductive, plique-à-jour is an enamelling technique, similar to cloisonné, but having the transparency of stained glass. First a design was outlined in metal (gold was often used), which was then attached to a sheet of copper, and filled in with enamels, which were fired to harden them. Finally, acid was added to dissolve the copper backing, resulting in the luminous enamel design. On the downside, plique-à-jour was a delicate process and required the steady and skilled hands of the best artisans, Lalique among them. Two shining examples are Lalique's ivory orchid brooch, page 77, and Edmond Becker's 'Belle de Nuit' brooch, seen here.

Art Nouveau ivory 'Belle de Nuit' brooch,
possibly by Edmond-Henri Becker,
French, c. 1900
Carved ivory figure, diamonds, plique-à-jour
enamel, platinum and silver-topped gold
This is surely one of the most dazzling works in ivory from this time. Night is represented as a female carved in ivory, her arms lifted as if she were about to leap into the night sky, her wings – more butterfly or bat than bird – the colour of twilight, expressed in plique-à-jour enamel, and the waning crescent moon and the stars in shimmering diamonds.

New Directions:
Union des Artistes Modernes

In the world of design, the year 1925 is one of those turning points when, as they say, everything changed. It was the year of the most important world expos in the most trend-setting of cities, the Exposition Internationale des Arts Décoratifs et Industriels Modernes in Paris. From that point forward, new designs were put forth, careers were launched, and the historical ripple effects continued to build throughout the twentieth century.

While the 1925 expo was making headlines, there were a handful of French designers and architects – members of the Société des Artistes – who viewed the ornamentation on display as excessive and overly decorative. They wanted none of it, and by 1929–30 an avant-garde splinter group had formed. This was the Union des Artistes Modernes (also known as the Modernes), whose members included René Herbst, Robert Mallet-Stevens, Jean Puiforcat, Charlotte Perriand, Raymond Templier, Gérard Sandoz, Jean Fouquet, Le Corbusier and Walter Gropius. The Modernes' manifesto was a passionate pronouncement of belief and instruction: 'Aesthete and art lover alike have today a primitive man's eye for material. Every time they come across intractability or limitations in it, they should measure its imaginative possibilities, comparing, where possible, the new and the old.... No other age has loved, as ours, all materials without exception, for themselves, for their nature, for their resistance to the artist's tools.'

The UAM was like a correction on a ship's navigation course, steering design to pure materials, to geometry and clean lines, and eventually to the shores of the Machine Age. By 1958, the Modernes had disbanded, but their nearly three-decade-long formation was a crucial gathering of talent and new directions.

When I walk through the streets, I see ideas everywhere for jewelry – wheels, cars, the machines of today. RAYMOND TEMPLIER

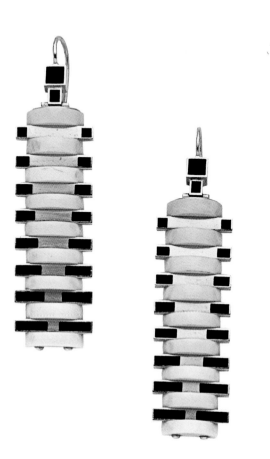

Ivory unicorn brooch,
by Verdura, American, c. 1945
Ivory, rubies, diamonds and 18K gold

*At first conjuring, the motif of the unicorn
recalls the medieval bestiary where the mythic
horned horse is held captive, subdued only by a
virginal maiden. Verdura's inspiration, however,
drew from more levity and gaiety: children's
carousels. His magnificent unicorn with its ruby
ruff is taken from the folk art wood carvings on
American carousels, whose origins date to Coney
Island in 1876, the country's largest amusement
park, and New York's Central Park, in 1908.*

Ivory statue/brooch, by Verdura, 1966
Carved ivory, diamonds, rubies
and 18K yellow gold

*There is something fun and refreshingly naive
about Verdura's figural objects – the swans whose
bodies swell with baroque shells, the diamond-
studded mice, the enamel and precious-stone-
studded snowmen. But the unicorns are truly
Verdura's pièce de résistance. This object is
yet another example of Verdura's imagination
– with a clever twist and turn, the unicorn's head
becomes a wearable brooch.*

Opposite
Art Deco ivory ear pendants,
by Raymond Templier, French, c. 1925
Ivory plaques, black lacquer and 18K gold

*Templier was among the early proponents
of simplicity inspired by the appealing
functionality of machines and their moving
parts, such as cogs and wheels. These earrings
are a superb example of Art Deco – geometric,
stacked, linear and, above all, modern.
Templier also made a similarly styled
brooch in circa 1927.*

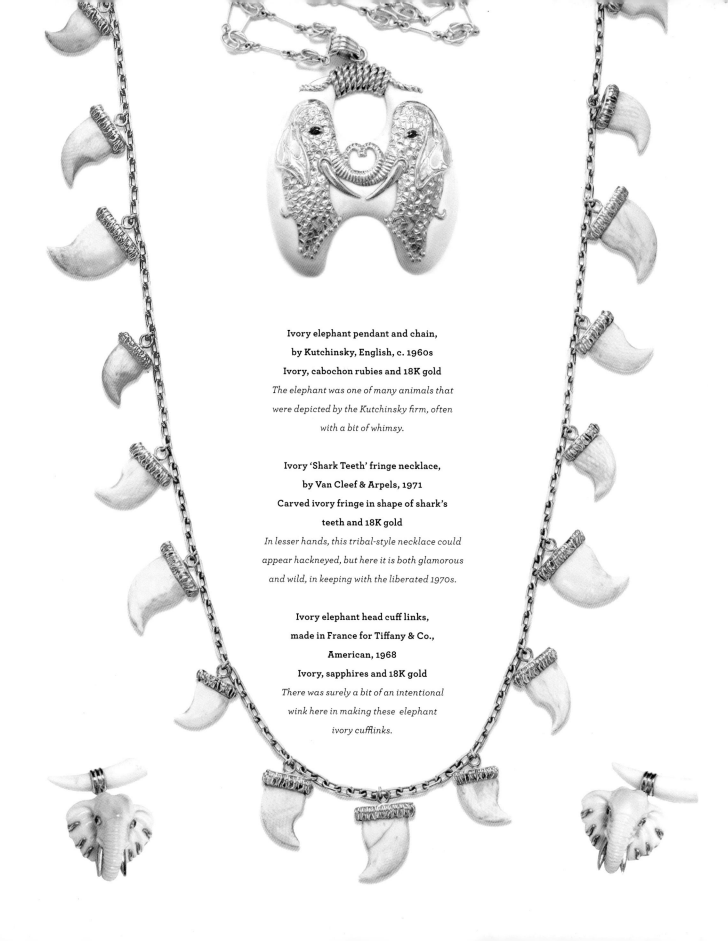

**Ivory elephant pendant and chain,
by Kutchinsky, English, c. 1960s
Ivory, cabochon rubies and 18K gold**
*The elephant was one of many animals that
were depicted by the Kutchinsky firm, often
with a bit of whimsy.*

**Ivory 'Shark Teeth' fringe necklace,
by Van Cleef & Arpels, 1971
Carved ivory fringe in shape of shark's
teeth and 18K gold**
*In lesser hands, this tribal-style necklace could
appear hackneyed, but here it is both glamorous
and wild, in keeping with the liberated 1970s.*

**Ivory elephant head cuff links,
made in France for Tiffany & Co.,
American, 1968
Ivory, sapphires and 18K gold**
*There was surely a bit of an intentional
wink here in making these elephant
ivory cufflinks.*

American Tastemakers

Three of the finest names in jewelry are Jean Schlumberger, Seaman Schepps and Tiffany & Company, and all can be claimed as American, if you consider that from 1956 onward Schlumberger was designing for Tiffany. Matters of residence and citizenship aside, each of these objects shows the popularity of figural forms, best expressed through the facile medium of ivory.

Ivory chessman knight brooch,
by Seaman Schepps, American, c. 1950s
Carved ivory, sapphires, rubies,
seed pearls and gold
This brave knight has reason to swagger:
he is one of Seaman Schepps's favourite motifs
from the mid-twentieth century, which the jeweler
embellished with colourful gemstones.

Ivory horse brooch,
by Tiffany & Co., American, c. 1940
Carved ivory, sapphires,
cabochon rubies, diamonds and gold
What couldn't Tiffany do? There is much to
admire in this little horse kitted out with such a
fine saddle. Even his hooves cry 'luxury'.

Ivory flower brooch,
by Jean Schlumberger, French, c. 1950
Ivory flowers, pink tourmalines and gold
It's as though a little fairy dust was sprinkled
on this creation, for an air of magic settles
comfortably on the petals and slender stems
of this cluster of spring flowers. Schlumberger
had a canny knack for taking the everyday
– a flower, a starfish, a bird – and making it
extraordinary and timeless.

Donald Claflin, Expressing Individual Taste

Ivory calla lily ear pendants, c. 1890

Ivory, diamonds and gold

'The calla lilies are in bloom again,' whispers a young Katharine Hepburn in the romantic comedy Stage Door *(1937). It was meant as a reference to the fading light, but over time it's been repeated as a gentle jibe at Hepburn's inimitable delivery of her lines.*

You don't get much more American than coming from a New England family who can date their descendants to the seventeenth century. Tiffany designer Donald Claflin had this impeccable stateside provenance, but how to account for the whimsy that permeated so much of his jewelry? There were walruses and hippos, dragons and ducks, turtles and frogs, many of them adapted from classic children's tales such as *Alice in Wonderland*. Alongside the humour, his work showed clear evidence of the jeweler who studied at the Parsons School of Design in New York and who for some years worked at David Webb before arriving at Tiffany in 1966. Like Webb, Claflin understood that the 1960s were like the fresh air that follows a rainstorm, in this case the rigidity and repression of the 1950s. Life in the sixties was looser – and becoming more so as the decade wore on – and the woman who could afford Claflin's jewelry wanted what fashion writer Suzy Menkes called 'jet-set luxury'. This was a new age of travel, and the resorts of the French Riviera and old stand-by's like Palm Beach oozed the laissez-faire life; money and morals weren't as tightly wound; and jewelry took up new partnerships with such natural materials as coral, ivory and exotic woods. Women were declaring their independence, and the saying 'life, liberty and the pursuit of happiness' rang with new meaning. Or as Donald Claflin said in 1968, 'This is a world where ... everything we do or wear expresses the individual, not someone else's idea of fashion.'

Opposite

Ivory brooch, by Donald Claflin for Tiffany & Co., American, 1968

Carved ivory, turquoise, sapphires, diamonds and 18K gold

Pierced ivory jewelry was among Claflin's achievements for Tiffany, where he worked from 1966 to 1977.

Nature is an endless source of renewal and people love having something of nature.

DONALD CLAFLIN

The Ivory Touch

Van Cleef & Arpels, Buccellati, David Webb... among the greatest names in jewelry, though each with very distinct profiles. What unites them here is their gently decorative touch with ivory: Webb's bangle looks like a pâtissier's handiwork, Buccellati's is more textural and fabric-like, in keeping with the house's fascination for textiles, and Van Cleef's bangle uses the fluting in the ivory as the design direction for the entire piece.

Ivory bangle, by Buccellati,
Italian, c. 1965
Ivory, cabochon emeralds, rubies and 18K gold
The work of this family-run company, which
opened in Milan in 1919, is all about details and
mastery of the ornate.

Ivory bangle, by Van Cleef & Arpels,
French, 1973
Ivory, rubies, diamonds and 18K gold
Elegant, dressy, and just tailored enough
even for daytime.

Ivory bangle, by David Webb,
American, c. 1960s
Ivory, cabochon rubies and emeralds,
and 18K gold
An exceptionally understated piece for Webb,
though entirely sumptuous. The whorls
of ivory are like whipped cream, and the
cabochon rubies and emeralds glisten like
sugared candy. A sublime triumph.

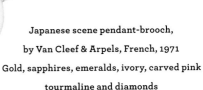

Ivory ear pendants,

by **Van Cleef & Arpels, French, c. 1970**

Ivory, sapphire, ruby, emerald,

diamond and 18K gold

Unexpected, and unexpectedly divine.

The design carries hints of the Far East.

Japanese scene pendant-brooch,

by **Van Cleef & Arpels, French, 1971**

Gold, sapphires, emeralds, ivory, carved pink

tourmaline and diamonds

In 1974 Van Cleef & Arpels became the first

French jewelry firm to have a location in Japan

when it opened a boutique in Tokyo.

Van Cleef & Arpels,
A Flair for the Foreign

An advertisement for Van Cleef & Arpels from 1922 shows a young woman bedecked in jewelry spinning a globe, its circumference fetchingly dotted by a strand of pearls: 'The world,' the ad seems to suggest, 'is at your fingertips.' So, too, the subtext reads, are the glories of this venerable house. Since its establishment in 1906, Van Cleef & Arpels has made jewelry history, a good deal of it in response to world events. If you know your history and geography, you too can spin a globe and map some important events by looking at the firm's many splendid jewels. Exploration, excavation, a taste for the exotic: each of these has resulted in jewelry motifs throughout the company's history. The discovery in Egypt of King Tutankhamen's tomb, the debut of the Ballets Russes in Paris, Beijing's Summer Palace, visits to and from Indian maharajas as well as Indian Independence in 1947 – each has led to important creations in colourful gemstones and shapes. The influence of the East – India, China and Japan – can be seen over the years in such motifs as dragons, Buddhas, peacocks and pagodas, as well as a taste for such stones and finishes as coral, jade, lapis, rubies, emeralds, gold leaf and black lacquer. Since 1922, when the firm designed jewelry for the maharajas of Nepal, Hyderabad, Nawanagar, Indore and Kapurthala, or when Japonisme and Art Nouveau were so influential, Van Cleef & Arpels has shown a flair for what is foreign, translating it with Gallic style and luxury.

Edith Head and Elizabeth Taylor: A Charmed Friendship

Edith Head cut a striking figure in the Hollywood world of costume designers and in many ways came to define the American film world's Golden Era. She won more Oscars than any other woman, and was nominated a record-breaking thirty-five times for her costume design over five decades. Her best-known work includes the iconic films *All About Eve* (1941), *A Place in the Sun* (1951) and *Sabrina* (1954). She dressed such great leading ladies as Ingrid Bergman and Barbara Stanwyck, but it was her work with Elizabeth Taylor that led to an especially close friendship between the two women. For years Edith Head collected Victorian theatre tickets made of ivory and eventually made a necklace of them. When she died in 1981, she left it to Dame Elizabeth, who has said that the necklace charms 'were always jingling, so stylish and so Edith, with her tiny upright body and her little strut'.

Gold and ivory necklace,

18th and 19th centuries

13 circular antique ivory opera passes and gold link chain

From Edith Head's Hollywood, *an autobiography by the great American film costumer and friend of Elizabeth Taylor: 'I fell in love with Elizabeth immediately. The reason is totally unrelated to films: I love animals and so does she.'*

Earrings, by Paolo Costagli, Italian, 2000

Mammoth ivory, Santos palisander rosewood and diamonds

Mammoth ivory allows Paolo Costagli to pursue his love of working with natural materials, though in very grand and special ways.

'Ebony and ivory live together in perfect harmony...'

Sometimes inspiration comes from the everyday, and for Paolo Costagli that meant his daily cappuccino. 'I was looking at my coffee, dark brown and beige, and I think to myself this colour is so pleasant, so warm and so nice. What can I do that is also a wearable combination of these colours? I looked at what I had and I found these warm, chocolatey tops. I was also listening to Paul McCartney and Stevie Wonder singing "Ebony and Ivory", and it all came together. I also wanted a little sparkle to cheer up the piece and that's why I added the diamonds.'

Patricia Von Musulin:
The Cerebral Sensualist

Whether you've seen one piece of jewelry by Patricia Von Musulin or many, the impression is the same: the work is emphatic, graphic, cerebral. It is also – from the smallest dabs of ivory earrings to Lucite bangles and necklaces strung with cubes of coral or onyx or jade – highly sensual. The impulse to stroke, fondle and touch the jewelry is part of its seduction: the tactility simply wins you over. So does the intelligence and vision. For more than two decades, Patricia Von Musulin's primary choice of materials has been constant: wood, ivory, silver and Lucite. A selection of semi-precious stones such as coral, jade, onyx and turquoise, as well as amber and unusual pearls may appear, but those four building blocks are always present somewhere. The other distinguishing feature of this jewelry is its retelling of architectural forms: look, for example, at the decorative swirls done in ivory or Lucite and you'll recognize the capital of a Corinthian column; even the artist's signature motif – an androgynous classical figure shown in profile – has hair that forms that same twirl at the end, a sort of stylized curl that is anything but 'cute'. Other examples abound: a silver cuff could be an archway or viaduct, a scored clasp could be paving stones. Patricia Von Musulin's father was an architect and her first piece of jewelry was influenced by Noguchi, so none of this comes as a surprise. Neither does the fact that prior to creating jewelry Patricia Von Musulin worked in industrial design and fashion. It has been in fashion, especially when shown with clothes by the dedicated modernist Geoffrey Beene or Perry Ellis, that Patricia Von Musulin's jewelry best reveals its couture nature. Then again, 'couture nature' is an apt phrase to describe Patricia Von Musulin and also her jewelry.

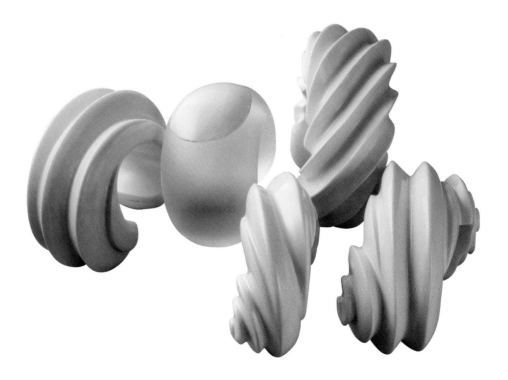

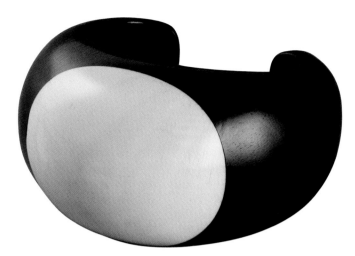

**'Ebony Dot' cuff and 'XOXO'
earrings, by Patricia Von Musulin,
American, c. mid-1980s
Hand-carved ebony and ivory**

*Studying the different dots and circles qualifies
as a lesson in scale. The 'XOXO' earrings suggest
the influence of the Wiener Werkstätte,
which is not surprising given that the
artist is of Austrian descent.*

**Ivory cuffs, by Patricia Von Musulin,
American, c. 1980s
Hand-carved ivory, sterling silver,
and bird's eye maple**

*Although the ivory is worked into various
shapes, the overall emphasis remains ardently
modernist. From left to right, 'Overpass' cuff,
'Now Voyager' ivory cuff with sterling silver
studs, 'Ivory Twist' cuff, and 'Ivory Twist' cuff
with bird's-eye maple wood insets and dowel.*

Opposite
**Ivory and Lucite cuffs, by Patricia
Von Musulin, American, 1979–84
Hand-carved ivory and frosted Lucite**

*Each cuff has a name – from left to right, 'Ridged',
'Dot', 'Medium Ram's Head', 'Kinsky' and 'Large
Ram's Head' – and in total shows four styles that
recur in Patricia Von Musulin's work – Bubble,
Twist, Ridged and Swirl. No mechanical means
of copying or reproduction are used; instead,
each piece is unique, crafted by hand and judged
by eye to conform in size and shape to others
in the series.*

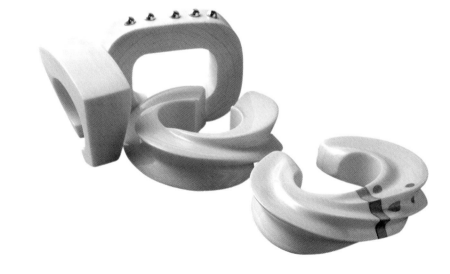

'Clown Collar' ivory necklace,
by Jill Burkee, 1979
Ivory, 22K gold, emeralds,
rubies and sapphires
*Talking heads carry on a six-way conversation
in this necklace; the introduction of the
Elizabethan cartwheel ruff, both ornamental
and functional, completes the artist's emphasis
on gesture and pattern, what she calls 'a woven
rhythm of communication'. Gianmaria Buccellati
designed and created the gold-link engraved
chain inset with the precious stones.*

'Tortoise' cuff,

by Ted Muehling, American, 2009

Carved mammoth ivory

The faceting of this cuff is a geometric

shrine to the possibilities and pleasure

of working with mammoth ivory.

Ivory 'Whatever' bangle, by Jessica Kagan

Cushman, American, 2008

Ivory with scrimshaw carving

As an art form, scrimshaw's heyday dates to

the 1800s in New England, when sailors aboard

whaling ships would carve images of their

journeys at sea into whale bone or teeth. Jessica

Cushman takes this traditional craft but applies

it with witty phrases from movies, literature or

current slang, resulting in what she describes

as 'somewhere between a tattoo and

a bumper sticker'. Other expressions

include 'We'll always have Paris', 'Lions

and tigers and bears, oh my!' and, best, 'Does

this bracelet make me look fat?'

Mammuthus Primigenus: The Wild 'n' Woolly Mammoth

If you could time travel back roughly four million years ago and journey to what is now Siberia and Alaska, you would have had a good chance of encountering one of the largest mammals ever to have roamed the earth: the woolly mammoth. This great beast, up to 14 feet tall (4 metres) and on average weighing 6 to 8 tons – adult males tipped the scale at 10 to 12 tons – had massive curlicue tusks, nearly 16 feet (5 metres) long. These large, looping tusks did actual spadework: the herbivore hunter used his tusks to scrape away at the ice underfoot in search of food.

Despite the great swath of time that separates them, the woolly mammoth is in fact related to the modern Indian elephant, though the former was as much as five times the weight of the African elephant, with considerably smaller ears. It belonged to the genus *Mammuthus*, a member of the elephant family, and the order *Probiscidea*. Scientists theorize that the mammoth died out toward the end of the last Ice Age (the date of its extinction varies), some 10,000 years ago. Over the course of its existence, it seems this shaggy, red-haired creature was a bit of a wanderer, having journeyed from Africa into Europe, and then along the Bering Strait into North America during the Early Pleistocene period, 1.8 to 1.5 million years ago.

What caused its extinction? Perhaps the same things that threaten the world today: climate change (what we now term global warming) and overhunting by humans. Ironically, it is the melting of ice and tundra in the Siberian permafrost, along with selective digging, that reintroduces the remarkably preserved mammoth and its twirl-shaped tusks.

5.

Pearls,
The Leading Ladies
of Jewelry

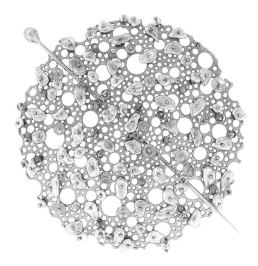

earls begin as sentiment and result in style. The stops along this transformation are what make them the leading ladies of jewelry, though more Ginger Rogers than Joan Crawford, more companionable than centre stage, which perhaps explains why anyone anywhere looks good in pearls, even if you're Chanel and mix in a few fake ones with the real thing. (Or if you're Audrey Hepburn in *Breakfast at Tiffany's* and your much-admired pearl necklace is more faux than fine.) Consider some of the names we have come to associate with these lustrous beauties: Consuelo Vanderbilt (later, the Duchess of Marlborough), Josephine Baker, the Duchess of Windsor, Grace Kelly, Her Majesty Queen Elizabeth II, Jacqueline Kennedy Onassis, Elizabeth Taylor, Diana, Princess of Wales, Audrey Hepburn, Eleanor Roosevelt, Coco Chanel, Michelle Obama. A more varied list would be hard to find, and yet this is what distinguishes the allure of pearls, for they are naturally accommodating and make every woman who wears them shine.

A taste for pearls usually begins in childhood – their sentimental home base – when a young girl's first piece of jewelry is typically pearls, such as the traditional 'add-a-pearl' necklace. Or a gift of pearls may come a little later, say on her sixteenth birthday, a college graduation, a marriage. On all these occasions pearls are ceremony markers, hence burnishing their appeal as beloved objects of personal esteem. Indeed, in any family pearls are one of the time-tested gifts that pass from generation to generation, mother to daughter, the feeling being that while one may *buy* emeralds or diamonds one always *inherits* pearls. Pearls, the unspoken rule goes, stay in the family.

At their simplest, pearls convey effortless beauty. They don't add style, they enhance it, and that is their secret arsenal in matters of dress. Queen Elizabeth I knew this, and when her gowns were massed in pearls, and she was adorned in them, they made her stature more imperious and grand. Grace Kelly's wedding attire likewise emphasized pearls, including a dress consisting of thousands of seed pearls sewn onto Valenciennes rose point lace, tulle and silk taffeta. In her case they symbolized a rite of passage, from commoner to aristocrat, from actress to princess. Although Prince Rainier had given her a stunning pearl and diamond suite from Van Cleef & Arpels as an engagement present, it was a simple pair of family pearl earrings she wore that day in 1956 that symbolized the purity of her entrée into royalty.

When it comes to the creation of a pearl, the path to greatness is paved with something like sand. 'Make love not war' could be the slogan for the pearl-producing mollusk (phylum *Mollusca*). Call it an irritant, call it *schmutz*, but whatever this foreign substance is that invades the shell of this mollusk (marine biologists now doubt that it is sand), the bivalve immediately sets to work to neutralize it, to make it more friend than foe, through the production of nacre. In the shell world, the breeder of pearls is the bivalve, which includes clams, scallops, mussels and oysters, its nacreous membrane what we call mother-of-pearl. In response to the invading troublemaker, nacre is secreted, layer upon layer, almost like an onion if you were to see it magnified, until the trespasser is thoroughly tranquillized by this process of encapsulation. *Et voilà*, a pearl is formed. In natural pearls this is always the result of chance; in cultivated pearls, industry plays matchmaker, with harvests guaranteed. A third group are the blister pearls, which grow attached to the inside wall of the shell; these can also be either natural or cultivated. Among all types, there are two further divisions depending on the body of water they inhabit, salt and fresh. But when many of us think of pearls, we think of subtle colour, with *lustre* common to all. Iridescence is also part of the pearl panoply, and it is often the combination of the core colour and its iridescence that gives a pearl its legendary shimmer.

As for identifying the designer who has most distinguished him or herself with pearls, that is like trying to say which chef makes the best roast chicken – pearls are a fundamental staple in the canon of every great jeweler, and always bear the signature style of their maker. For every woman, as well, it is that 'signature style' which among her jewelry makes pearls her most loyal friends.

A Mania for Motifs

Motifs invoke so many associations – religious, geographic, cultural, symbolic and ceremonial. Most broadly they play into that big decorator sandbox called ornament.

Pearl knot brooch, English, c. 1890

Natural pearls, diamonds and gold

The clinician might describe a love knot as a tied bow, but anyone with a drop of red blood knows it means much more – love, commitment, betrothal, lasting or eternal love, all the glories of harmony.

In this particular brooch there is so much movement it is as though life itself were coursing through the myriad swells and curves.

Swag necklace, French, c. 1880

Pearls, diamonds and silver-topped gold

The garland style was decidedly feminine and delicate, and suited the lowered décolletage in women's finery.

Fringe necklace, c. 1880

Pearls, diamonds and silver-topped gold

'Round as the globe upon which we live, they [pearls] will probably be worn and appreciated as long as life exists upon this sphere.'
—George Frederick Kunz, Tiffany gemologist

Victorian (or Edwardian?)
stylized bloom necklace, English?, c. 1890
Natural pearls, diamonds and 15K gold
The delicacy of the stylized blooms and
use of pearls in combination with diamonds
are in keeping with jewelry made
at the close of the 1800s.

Necklace, late 19th century
Pearls, cultured pearls (2) and platinum
It's beautiful, it's delicate, and it was first owned
by Julia Dent Grant, wife of Ulysses S. Grant,
America's 18th president. Whereas Grant came
by his military might through on-the-job training,
his spouse was altogether a natural at whatever
came her way, including serving as First Lady
in 1869. Among her contemporaries she was
admired for her dress, including her fine jewelry,
which might have included this necklace.
It was eventually passed on to the Grants'
eldest granddaughter, Julia Grant,
Princess Cantacuzène.

The Dog Collar and Queen Alexandra: Creating a Royal Trend

When does fashion move into that timeless arena called style? When does a popular look become a standard? Such was the influence of Queen Alexandra, daughter-in-law of the great Queen Victoria, who with many fine royal jewels at her command, chose to wear multiple strands of them clasped around her neck, thus creating a mini tidal wave of thirst for the *collier de chien*, or dog collar. Naturally beautiful and high-necked, the Queen might have caused ripples among the fashion-conscious no matter what she wore, but the collar became her signature look and can be seen in official portraits of her over the many years of her life as a royal. (The unspoken purpose of the Queen's pearl-covered chokers was to cover a childhood scar.) Reason aside, this tight-fitting necklace with its many strands (typically five to seven though sometimes as many as nine), was part of the Queen's finery, and since its debut has remained in style.

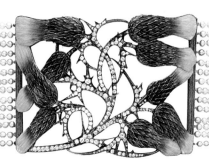

Art Nouveau thistle dog collar, by René Lalique, French, c. 1900
Seed pearls, diamonds, enamel and gold
The emphasis is on the decorative plaque depicting sycamore seedpods, but this time Lalique has chosen to mount it within a seed pearl choker, fashionable from the mid-1800s up to World War I.

Multi-strand natural pearl bracelet, by Cartier, French, 1915
Natural pearls, diamonds and platinum-topped gold
Nothing is sweeter than the gentle cascade of pearls on your wrist – there's a bit of movement, a lot of shimmer, and an overall lightness, to which even the pavé diamond spacers add.

Dog collar, c. 20th century
Pearls, emerald, diamonds and silver-topped gold
With their inherent iridescence, pearls are natural floodlights against a woman's skin, and when worn close to the face as on a dog collar, the effects can be dazzling.

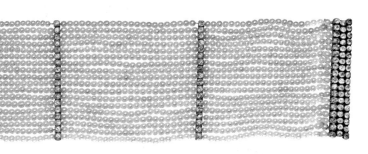

Bodice Ornament, by Tiffany & Co.,
American, 1890–95
Platinum, gold, diamonds and conch pearls
Everything about this brooch expresses the
best in jewelry at this time, from its design to its
materials. Bodice ornaments were fashionable
during the latter years of the nineteenth century,
with bows and swags frequent motifs. Diamonds
were newly available to the wealthy American,
having been a rarity on the market until this
period; and conch pearls have always been
highly prized. The seven conch pearls – ranging
from blushing pink to a deeply saturated pink
– were specially selected by Tiffany's renowned
gemologist, George Frederick Kunz. The central
conch may be removed and worn as a pendant.

Brooch, c. 1890
Pearls, diamonds, gold and silver
Simplicity and refinement: the domed pearl is a
mabe, and the drop is a natural saltwater pearl.

Natural pearl and diamond spray brooch,
c. 20th century
Natural pearls, diamonds, silver and gold
This delicate brooch is a modern-made piece
with the look of an earlier vintage.

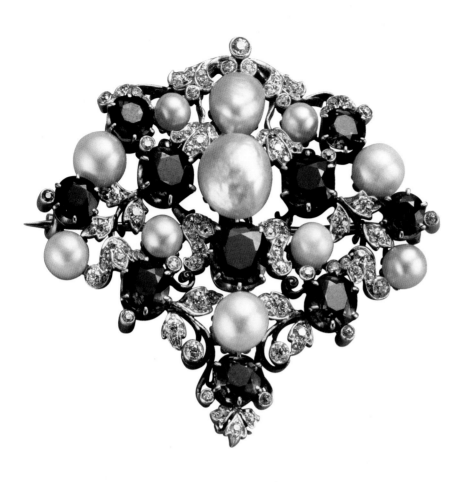

Below

Edwardian brooch, by Marcus & Co., c. 1900

Baroque pearl, multi-coloured pearls,

diamonds, plique-à-jour enamel and 18K gold

Marcus & Co. cleverly picked up on the nuances
of the baroque pearl by accenting it with these
four variously coloured pearls, all of them in
shades of the aubergine or eggplant family.

Above

Brooch, by G. Paulding Farnham,

American, 1899

American freshwater pearls, Montana

sapphires, diamonds, platinum,

enamel and 18K gold

'Made in America' is an apt description of this
spectacular Tiffany & Co. brooch. The sapphires
came from the region of Yogo Gulch in Montana,
and the freshwater pearls from Wisconsin and
Tennessee. This piece was created by one of
Tiffany's greatest and earliest designers, and
his name deserves to be better known. He is
Paulding Farnham, who for two decades at the
turn of the twentieth century made some of the
most beautiful jewelry in America.

Pearl pendant, English, 1900
Baroque pearl, diamonds, rubies and platinum

The word 'baroque' describes the gamut of irregularly shaped pearls. Baroque pearls have long fascinated both the jeweler and the wearer, and the ever-present dilemma is simply what to make with them. In this case, abstraction won out, though the massing of diamond-and-ruby flowers provides additional textural layering and complexity. This fabulous creation is entirely unapologetic – it claims to be nothing more than itself, take it or leave it.

Above right
Turtle brooch, by Marcus & Co.,
American, 1910
Pearl, diamonds, demantoid garnets
and platinum-topped 18K yellow gold

Just about the prettiest turtle to be mounted in jewelry is this exquisite Edwardian brooch made by the American firm Marcus & Co., founded by Henry Marcus and his son William in 1892. The jewelry world was even more tightly knit then than now, and though the elder Marcus twice worked for Tiffany & Co., the two companies became chief rivals.

Turtle brooch, Vienna?, c. 1885
Natural pearl, cushion-cut diamond,
gold and platinum

If you've never stroked a turtle before, this might be the one to change your mind, for his head, neck and back are a silken slab of natural pearl, its contours perfectly capturing his slightly domed physique. The remaining turtle features are formed from European-cut pavé diamonds set in platinum and gold. This particular style was a speciality of the Austro-Hungarian Empire.

Swan brooch, c. 1860
Baroque blister pearl, diamonds,
gold and silver
*'He did not himself know what to do. He was
more than happy, yet none the prouder: for a
good heart is never proud. He remembered
how he had been pursued, and made game of;
and now he heard everybody say he was the
most beautiful of all beautiful birds. . . . He
then flapped his wings, and raised his slender
neck, as he cried, in the fullness of his heart: "I
never dreamed such happiness while I was an
ugly duckling."' —Hans Christian Andersen,
'The Ugly Duckling'*

Art Nouveau egret brooch, c. 1900
Freshwater pearl?, enamel, ruby,
diamonds and 9K gold
*In the nineteenth century the Great Egret's
feathers were prized for women's hats, a
fancy that nearly decimated the mighty bird's
population in North America. It has since
happily come under the protection of the
National Audubon Society.*

Flamingo brooch, American, c. 1930
Mississippi River pearl and diamonds

Opposite
Lyrebird brooch, c. late 19th century
Baroque pearl, diamonds, feathers and gold
*This is the Superb Lyrebird (Menura superba),
picked out in pearls, diamonds and actual
feathers. Around the same time as this brooch
was made, ornithologists John and Elizabeth
Gould were preparing their book Birds of
Australia, which included this unusually
upright winged bird.*

Pearl Lengths – Standards of Design

Collier de chien or dog collar—12 to 13 inches (30 to 33 cm); a multi-strand necklace that fits snugly at mid-neck; made popular by Queen Alexandra, consort to King Edward VII, who wore this style of pearl necklace for years, presumably to hide a childhood neck scar.

Choker—14 to 16 inches (35 to 40 cm); a fairly short necklace in which the necklace sits at the top of the collar bone; formal portraits of Grace Kelly often show her wearing a pearl choker.

Princess—17 to 19 inches (43 to 48 cm); this single strand is an all-purpose length and ideal for the addition of a pendant.

Matinee—20 to 26 inches (50 to 66 cm); with a bit more swing than the Princess, but more conservative than the Opera.

Opera—26 to 36 inches (66 to 91 cm); can be worn as one long strand (think Chanel) or doubled.

Sautoir or rope—40 to 48 inches (100 to 120 cm); the grandest length for pearls; Queen Mary, consort to King George V, was renowned for her imaginative ways of wearing sautoirs, a trait passed down to her daughter, Queen Alexandra, who also wore pearl sautoirs along with a pearl *collier de chien*.

**Three-strand necklace,
c. late 20th century
Multi-coloured baroque pearls,
ruby, diamonds and white gold**
*By any standard, this is a stunning
and unusual strand of baroque pearls.
It had been owned by actress Ellen Barkin,
adding further luster to the pearls.*

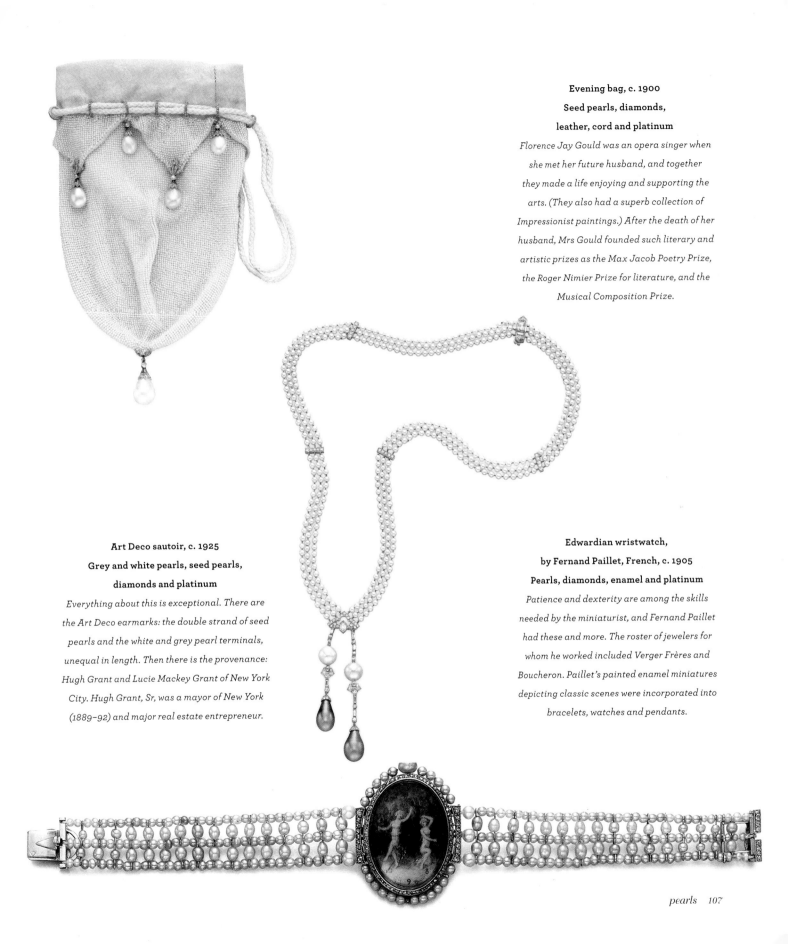

Evening bag, c. 1900
Seed pearls, diamonds,
leather, cord and platinum

Florence Jay Gould was an opera singer when she met her future husband, and together they made a life enjoying and supporting the arts. (They also had a superb collection of Impressionist paintings.) After the death of her husband, Mrs Gould founded such literary and artistic prizes as the Max Jacob Poetry Prize, the Roger Nimier Prize for literature, and the Musical Composition Prize.

Art Deco sautoir, c. 1925
Grey and white pearls, seed pearls,
diamonds and platinum

Everything about this is exceptional. There are the Art Deco earmarks: the double strand of seed pearls and the white and grey pearl terminals, unequal in length. Then there is the provenance: Hugh Grant and Lucie Mackey Grant of New York City. Hugh Grant, Sr, was a mayor of New York (1889–92) and major real estate entrepreneur.

Edwardian wristwatch,
by Fernand Paillet, French, c. 1905
Pearls, diamonds, enamel and platinum

Patience and dexterity are among the skills needed by the miniaturist, and Fernand Paillet had these and more. The roster of jewelers for whom he worked included Verger Frères and Boucheron. Paillet's painted enamel miniatures depicting classic scenes were incorporated into bracelets, watches and pendants.

Multi-strand necklace, c. 1870

Pearls, diamonds, gold and silver

Evergreens of the jeweler's repertoire are the
diamond ring and the pearl necklace. One
is a deal clincher whereas the other is also
declarative but well mannered, a whisper rather
than a shout. Pearls, regardless of size, are
always in good taste. To quote from
The In and Out Book by Robert Benton
and Harvey Schmidt, 'A Clean Girl is an
IN Girl.' And clean girls wear pearls.

Art Deco vanity case,

by Van Cleef & Arpels, French, 1925

Gold, natural pearls, black lacquer

and diamonds

Florence Jay Gould owned this elegant vanity
case. Upon her death in 1993 the Florence Gould
Foundation was created to support French–
American causes in the arts.

Art Deco tassel pendant,

by Cartier, French, c. 1918

Pearls, diamonds and platinum

One could be forgiven for coveting
this perfect tassel.

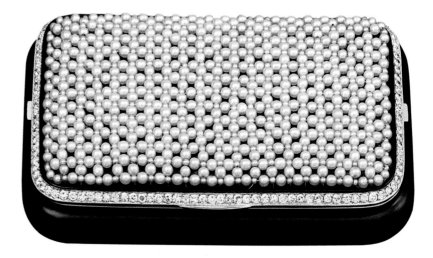

Daisy, you know that I love you. You're worth a three hundred thousand dollar pearl necklace to me. F. SCOTT FITZGERALD, THE GREAT GATSBY, 1925

**Bunch of grapes brooch,
by Van Cleef & Arpels, French, c. 1915**
Gold, silver, natural pearls and diamonds
*A rarely seen and altogether stunning debut
among the earliest of all jewels by Van Cleef
& Arpels. Here the rich range of pearl colours is
used to suggest the natural hues of grapes.
For connoisseurs of jewelry, this is a remarkable
piece of execution and beauty.*

The Pearl Bow Brooch

A surmount on a brooch featuring a ribbon bow was among the popular motifs of Edwardian jewelry, characterized by the lightness of platinum and the beauty of pearls. Around the time these brooches were in vogue, the market for pearls had soared beyond all reason. In New York, robber baron Morton F. Plant had a severe case of pearl fever: in 1917 he traded his 5th Avenue home to Pierre Cartier for the French jeweler's two-strand pearl necklace. Its 128 pearls at that time were valued at one million dollars.

Right

Edwardian bow brooch,

by Cartier, French?, c. 1900

Pearls, diamonds and platinum-topped gold

By the time Mrs Cornelius Vanderbilt acquired this brooch, she and her husband were the new owners of the Breakers, the most impressive estate on Newport, Rhode Island, and of the smartest address in Manhattan, 1 West 57th Street. Alice Gwynne Vanderbilt, dubbed 'the Queen of New York society', was one of the wealthiest women in New York (or anywhere else, for that matter), and maintained her dominion with what Hans Nadelhoffer calls a 'fin-de-siècle aesthetic' inspired by the theatrical style of France's Court of Versailles. Cartier, which had opened an American branch in New York in 1909, was a loyal supplier of jewelry to Mrs Vanderbilt, including this piece, whose pearl tassel flares out just like a bell.

Edwardian bow brooch, c. 1905

Pearls, diamonds and platinum

A celebration of the pearl dominates the feeling of this luminous brooch, massed with a particularly sensitive graduation of the pearls on the bow.

Above left

Bow brooch, Boucheron, French, c. 1928

Natural pearl and diamonds

Curves have been lopped off, edges have been squared, and the linear Art Deco look has replaced the curlicue delicacy of the Edwardian style.

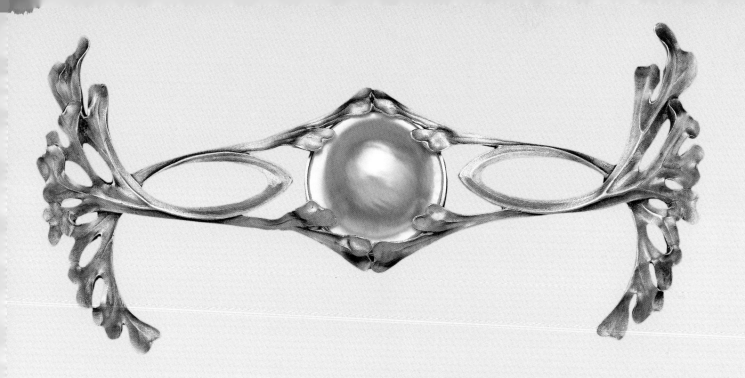

Art Nouveau seaweed brooch,
by Paul Liénard, c. 1908
Mabe pearl and gold

Liénard is known for the lustrous work
he did in horn and gentle cascades of pearls,
but he was equally drawn to seaweed motifs,
as in this Art Nouveau brooch.

Art & Crafts brooch, by Josephine
Hartwell Shaw, American, c. 1913
Blister pearls and gold

Two years after Bostonian Josephine Hartwell
Shaw, a leading figure in the city's Society of
Arts & Crafts, made this brooch, the painter
Cecilia Beaux said, 'I predict an hour when
the term "Women in Art" will be as strange
sounding a topic as "Men in Art" would be now.'
In America during the early decades of the
twentieth century, Shaw was making a name
for herself as a proponent of the movement in
jewelry that privileged natural or raw beauty
over manufactured beauty, unusual stones over
those more traditional. The hand of the artist
is the impetus here, not the gender.

**The Gulf Parure, by Harry Winston,
American, late 20th century**

Natural pearls, diamonds and platinum

*Even hyperbole doesn't do justice to the Gulf
Parure. Its magnificence can be measured in a
steady stream of facts: that it exists as a suite,
including a bracelet, detachable ear pendants,
and a ring; that it was commissioned from one
of the world's greatest jewelry houses, no doubt
using the original owner's pearls and diamonds;
and that in total it comprises 193 natural
saltwater pearls and 166 diamonds, of which 66
weigh nearly 160 carats. The size and quality of
the pearls alone make it one of the great parures
of the mid- to late twentieth century.*

Baroda, the Highest Standard

They are the Baroda pearls, the most important natural pearl necklace to have been offered at auction, and to connoisseurs those two words convey unparalleled excellence – provenance and history, quality and quantity, artistic brilliance. The facts speak for themselves: the Maharaja of Baroda, Khande Rao Gaekwar (r. 1856–1870), one of India's greatest collectors of jewelry and powerful leaders, acquired the original seven-strand suite of graduated natural pearls as part of the state jewels; today, this double-strand necklace is comprised of the most perfect and largest of the fourth, fifth, sixth and seventh rows of the original seven-strand necklace; there are sixty-eight graduated pearls, all of them natural; the clasp is a cushion-cut diamond made by Cartier; the ear pendants are natural pearls; the button pearl in the ring is natural. One last fact: in less than three minutes at auction in 2007, the suite sold for $7.1 million, a new record for pearls.

The Baroda Pearls, Indian, c. 19th century;
diamond necklace clasp by Cartier
Necklace, ear pendants, ring and brooch
Pearls, diamonds, platinum, gold and silver
In 1907, G. F. Kunz, gemologist for Tiffany & Co., examined the Baroda pearls. They are 'among the greatest jeweled treasures of India', he reported, and his analysis has stood for more than a century. They were also perhaps the most expensive jewelry owned by the Maharaja of Baroda, Khande Rao Gaekwar, one of the world's most important collectors of jewelry in the nineteenth century. His collection included the 'Star of the South' diamond, 129 carats, and the 'English Dresden', 78.53 carats, as well as the exemplary Baroda pearls en suite, probably gathered along India's southern coast. This necklace was created from the original seven-strand necklace.

A fool would know that with tweeds or other daytime clothes one wears gold and that with evening clothes one wears platinum. DUCHESS OF WINDSOR

'*Small Woman, Big Stones*'

Why is it the Duchess of Windsor had so much dash when she wore jewelry? She wasn't a classic beauty, she had a figure that was more skinny than svelte, and yet she possessed a je ne sais quoi style that clung to her like perfume. In 1947, she was number one on the International Best Dressed List Hall of Fame, the one throne she reigned from with panache and her ever-changing ensembles. As she wrote in her memoir, 'Mine is a simple story. It is the story of an ordinary life that became extraordinary.' Yet the Duchess of Windsor was inherently clever, a canny strategist of what fashion critic Suzy Menkes called 'the minor arts of exquisite living', which included dressing. (Both she and the Duke shared a penchant for finery *à table* as well as in their wardrobes.) She knew how to costume her thin frame with tailored clothes (think tight

waist, narrow shoulders), an unchanging hemline, and typically monochromatic colour schemes unless she was playing up the Palm Beach/Capri/Côte d'Azur look. Although she was the Label Lady of her day, it could be said that the Duchess revered not the god of cloth as much as the goddess of gold and baubles. Van Cleef & Arpels, Belperron, Verdura, David Webb, Harry Winston and Cartier, for whom she was a walking advertisement, were the jewelers she privileged, day and night, and for years. One friend remarked that the Duchess played with her jewelry the way a small child plays with her dolls – constantly, and with something bordering on obsession. But for all that has been said and written about the Duchess of Windsor, *New York* magazine, in 1987, had the simplest summation: 'Small woman, big stones.'

Ring, by Cartier, French, c. 1964

Natural pearl, diamonds and 18K gold

A common injunction from the Duchess:
'Watch my hands.' Although she owned many
fabulous rings, the Duchess was known to dislike
her hands, which she thought unbecoming.
In most formal portraits they are either
clenched, out of sight or gloved.

Necklace, by Van Cleef & Arpels, French, 1964

Cultured pearls, diamonds and gold

According to the Van Cleef & Arpels archives,
these pearls were strung specially
for the Duchess in 1964.

Above

Pair of turban ear clips,

by Cartier, French, c. 1943

Seed pearls, diamonds, platinum

and 18K gold

Amidst the vastness of her jewelry collection,
this particular pair of earrings was a natural
look for the Duchess of Windsor. The turban
design not only reflects the ancient headgear
form, but also in more abstract fashion calls
to mind the radial form of certain seashells,
another item worn with style by the Duchess
as seen in her many Webb shell ear clips.

Belperron Rings: A Signature Style

Everything that Suzanne Belperron designed had a perfection about it – she had an ability to come up with ideal forms, sometimes very simple, such as these rings, or more involved, such as the pearl cuff owned by the Duchess of Windsor. It was Belperron's ability to fuse the simple with the artful that made her an artist in her day and a cult figure now.

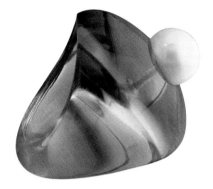

Bombé ring, by Suzanne Belperron,

French, c. 1940

Natural pearl, quartz and platinum

Architecture in a ring: the angles of the smoky quartz are a natural foil for the round pearl.

Ring, by Suzanne Belperron,

French, c. 1930s

Pearls and chalcedony

Most chalcedony used for jewelry is blue, but in fact it occurs naturally in such shades as pink and beige, too, as in this vertically stacked pearl ring.

Ring, by Suzanne Belperron,

French, c. 1930s

Pearl and chalcedony

The perfect ice-cream cone of Art Deco jewelry: a pearl dollop atop a swirl of chalcedony.

Elizabeth Taylor and La Peregrina, High-Calibre History

If you love pearls and tales of history and provenance, beauty and star power, then the story of Elizabeth Taylor and the Peregrina pearl necklace she owns is the crème de la crème. Since girlhood, Dame Elizabeth has adored jewelry, a passion shared equally with her husband Richard Burton, who had a natural eye for selecting excellent pieces for his wife. In 1969, at an auction held by Parke-Bernet in New York, Burton made a spectacular purchase: the Peregrina pearl, pear-shaped and perfect. Portions of its provenance were clear cut, other aspects less certain but altogether credible and tantalizing. The Peregrina dates from the sixteenth century, perhaps found at sea by a young slave, and had been owned by both Spanish and French royal households before making its way to Dame Elizabeth. At that point it was on a slender chain of intermittently spaced pearls. Three years later, the Peregrina received a facelift: working with designer Al Durante of Cartier, Dame Elizabeth decided to have it freshly mounted, in a style based in part on a necklace seen in a portrait of Mary, Queen of Scots. As the actress writes in her book, *Elizabeth Taylor, My Love Affair with Jewelry*: 'It was the most incredibly beautiful choker. But the little diamond bail, suspending the pearl, is original to the piece.' As is, of course, the pear-shaped pearl.

The Peregrina, early 16th century
Necklace, designed
by Elizabeth Taylor with Al Durante
of Cartier, American, c. 1972
Pearls, diamonds, rubies, platinum
and 18K gold

It is one of the world's most significant pear-shaped pearls, dating from the sixteenth century, and today it is owned and cherished by the great beauty and renowned jewelry collector Elizabeth Taylor. Along its four-hundred-year history, the Peregrina has been in Spain and France, always living in royal comfort. In keeping with the Peregrina's distinguished heritage – and like many women who change fine jewelry to suit their personality and style – Dame Elizabeth had a dramatic new setting made. How fitting that the Peregrina, which means wanderer, has found such a loving home in which to nest.

I feel as though I'm only the custodian of my jewelry. ELIZABETH TAYLOR

Bhagat, the Artisan Seeker of India

Viren Bhagat is a perpetual seeker. As he patiently tracks down Burmese rubies for a collar of diamonds and rubies, or places the finest of old emeralds with pearls, he is continually updating India's artistic tradition in jewelry. Inspiration for Bhagat comes from a celebrated period of India's past – the Mughal decorative arts of the sixteenth and seventeenth centuries, including the arts of Persia. Maybe the pattern of a carpet is detected in a jewelry clasp, or perhaps the shape of marble inlay from a temple turns up as a pendant; the retelling of style and influence is a signature component running through all of Bhagat's work. You might call this well-heeled jeweler the peacemaker of influences from throughout India and neighbouring countries, for in his flexible hands forms comingle without heed to politics or tribal and territorial clashes. Bhagat works exclusively with Indian gemstones and diamonds, and not only is he one of India's most-renowned jewelers, but his insistence on luxury and excellence has earned him a following among connoisseurs worldwide. As he says, 'My jewelry has subtle Indian references, but it's not ethnic.'

I love older stones; they have a different subtle charm, more like a whisper than a shout. VIREN BHAGAT

Lotus flower pendant necklace, by Viren Bhagat, Indian, c. 2007
Pearls, diamonds and platinum
Very few designers can take the best of older, formidable jewelry forms and make them feel new and modern. Viren Bhagat, however, is inspired by the challenge and succeeds brilliantly as in his adaptation of the pendant tassel necklace popular more than a century ago.

Famous Pearls

Pearls found, purchased, looted, inherited, or traded make for some of the liveliest (or darkest) tales in the jeweler's storybooks. Here are some of the classic pearls, the ones that top most lists when it comes to describing one of nature's greatest beauties.

Abernethy Pearl—44 grains; freshwater pearl found in Scotland in 1967.

Black Beauty—26.12 grains; button-shaped natural black pearl from South America.

Drexel Pearl—33.8 carats; natural Polynesian pearl, named after philanthropist Mary S. Irick Drexel; made into a Belle Epoque brooch by Cartier.

Hope Pearl—1,800 grains/450 carats; the most famous and largest of the natural saltwater pearls; a drop-shaped blister pearl, formerly owned by Henry Philip Hope, after whom it is named.

La Pellegrina—111 grains; pear-shaped, from the seventeenth century, at one time part of the Spanish Crown Jewels.

La Peregrina—203.84 grains/50 carats; one of the finest examples of a pear-shaped pearl; found by a slave in the sixteenth century and originally part of the Spanish Crown jewels; subsequent owners included the Bonaparte family in the early 1800s; purchased at auction in 1969 by Richard Burton for his wife, Elizabeth Taylor, who has since refashioned it and wears it to this day.

Pearl of Asia—2,400 grains/600 carats; one of the largest natural pearls in the world; found during the seventeenth century in India, it was later given to the Chinese Emperor Qianlong.

Pearl of Kuwait—257.41 grains/64.35 carats; given its shape, this natural pearl was named for the Persian Gulf region where it was thought to have been discovered in the nineteenth century; at one time the world's sixth largest pearl.

Queen Pearl—93 grains; a deep pink pearl found in Notch Brook, New Jersey, in 1857; purchased by Charles L. Tiffany and later sold to Princess Eugénie of France.

**Flower fringe necklace,
by Harry Winston, American,
c. late 20th century**
Cultured pearls, diamonds and 18K gold
Echoing the fringe style of the late 1800s, this Winston necklace is made au courant by the dynamic floral profile and gold setting.

Necklace and ear clips, by Bulgari,
Italian, c. 1970
Cultured pearls, carved coral petals, diamonds
and 18K gold

Bulgari's dressed-up version of that girlhood
staple, the daisy chain, this remarkable necklace
is composed of eighteen marguerite daisies
graduated in size, each blossom punctuated
at centre with a cultured pearl, and the petals
coated with pink coral.

Pearl brooch, by Schlumberger, c. 1955–60
Pearls, diamonds and gold

A life force seems to permeate every piece
made by the great Schlumberger: birds chirp,
butterflies quiver, feathers flutter. And why not
say this brooch is a flower, for it is the pearlescent
bloom of magnificence. With good reason
Tiffany & Co. wrote that their 'rarest treasure is a
genius called Schlumberger'.

Necklace, by Bulgari, Italian,
c. late 20th century
Cultured pearls, diamonds and 18K gold
*A Bulgari classic, showing strength,
beauty and confidence.*

Below
Pair of cultured pearl and gold ear pendants,
by Buccellati, Italian, late 20th century,
early 21st century
Cultured pearls, 18K white and yellow gold
*The airy design of these chandelier earrings
makes them easy companions to more
elaborate pearl-and-gold jewelry.*

Flower brooch, c. 1950
Elongated freshwater pearls,
diamonds and 18K gold
*Sometimes fireworks are just like
this brooch: flowers bursting into full bloom,
their starry trails like cascades of diamonds
glittering in the night air.*

Coco Chanel, the Oracle and Oxymoron of Fashion

There is a sort of opiate cloud that surrounds the subject of Chanel and fashion, obfuscating what Chanel herself perhaps most disdained, the *truth*. She was the queen of cunning, a nimble assembler of story and truth, and while in her later years Chanel sought to burnish her influence by tossing out bons mots the way rice is thrown at weddings, those around her were likewise compelled to comment on her life and work. Everyone, it seems, has tried to decipher and define fashion's eternal enigma.

POIRET: *'She was poverty deluxe.'*
CHANEL: *'Dress shabbily and they remember the dress; dress impeccably and they remember the woman.'*
CECIL BEATON: *'Chanel's personality, like her designs,*
was something of a paradox, a mingling of the masculine and intensely feminine.'
CHANEL: *'I invented my life by taking for granted that everything I did not like would have an opposite, which I would like.'*
KARL LAGERFELD: *'For a woman who tried to create a revolution in the beginning, she later became the most classic person in the world.'*
CHANEL: *'Scheherezade is easy; a little black dress is difficult.'*
JEAN COCTEAU: *'the marvellous little head of a black swan'.*
CHANEL: *'Jewelry isn't meant to make you look rich, it's meant to adorn you, and that's not the same thing.'*

'Matelassé' necklace, by Chanel,
French, c. late 20th century
Cultured pearls, diamonds and 18K gold
As Dior famously remarked of Chanel, 'With a black pullover and 10 rows of pearls, she revolutionized fashion.'

'Matelassé' ring (top) and pair of ear clips,
by Chanel, French, c. late 20th century
Cultured pearls, diamonds and 18K gold
Her biography is almost as compelling as her designs and famous quips, but the true measure of Chanel's impact is that it never seems to wane. Or if it does, like the moon it waxes again. Chanel was, and is, the designer every woman seems to know and measure herself against.

Bracelet, by John Donald, English, 1968
Multi-coloured baroque
cultured pearls and 18K gold
The nicely chunky gold setting is offset
by the Easter-egg colours of these baroque
pearls, a balance achieved through John
Donald's sensitive eye for proportion and form.

Ring, by John Donald, English, 1976
Cultured baroque pearl and 18K gold
'Molten' is a word often used to describe
the effect of John Donald's gold work.

Brooch, by John Donald, English, 1969
Cultured baroque pearl and 18K gold
In John Donald's words, his jewelry is
'baroque in mood and essentially
organic in form'.

The Natural World of John Donald

Adjectives about John Donald come easily, though they all require a one-word password: *appreciation*. To understand this English goldsmith and jeweler is to appreciate that he is independent, irreverent, uninhibited, thoughtful, experimental, romantic, inspired, unconventional. If he bows to a greater force it is the natural world, for organic materials dominate his entire oeuvre. The first significant viewing of his work was at the groundbreaking 'Modern Jewelry' show launched by Goldsmiths' Company in 1961. What did people see? A man who found fluid ways to work gold in combination with precious and semi-precious stones, often shown unfaceted. His jewelry, notable for unusual settings, quickly set a new standard for what fine jewelry could be, but without the steady diet of 'the tried and true'. Now stones might swing or float on thin gold wires or nest in gold craters, and instead of perfect circles, squares or rectangles, asymmetry reigned. For John Donald, the irregular became regular, and for anyone with a good eye and an open mind, Donald's jewelry was a fresh way to show status that wasn't stuffy. The man who was part of ushering in Britain's Modern Jewelry movement a half-century ago is now accorded the respect of having created a lasting heritage in fine jewelry.

**Pearl necklace and ear pendants,
by Andrew Grima, English, c. 1972
Cultured baroque pearls,
gold and diamonds**

*When you take in the long view of twentieth-
century jewelry, you come to Andrew Grima and
then you come to a full stop: there was no one else
like him. It wasn't just the emphasis on nature, or
of using natural materials at their organic best,
or of cleverly constructing pieces that seemed to
suit the period. Grima was larger than the time
in which he lived, for no matter what medium he
worked in there was a thoughtfulness of purpose
and idea, and application of technique that
made him a master.*

'Keshi Cocktail' ear pendants,
by Marilyn Cooperman, American, 2006
Keshi pearls, coloured
diamonds and 18K gold

Before she designed jewelry, Marilyn Cooperman
worked in fashion, which shows in these earrings.
Though they are contemporary, they would be
right at home in such film classics from 1968
as The Thomas Crown Affair *or* The Swimmer,
where women looked jazzy and zippy whether
they were at a glamorous party or having drinks
alone poolside. In other words, these earrings
swing, much like the high-octane
sixties and seventies.

'Botticelli' brooch, by Marilyn Cooperman,
American, 2005
Multi-coloured baroque cultured pearls,
coloured diamonds and 18K gold

For such an urban creature, there's something of
the natural world in Marilyn Cooperman's work,
including the names for a variety of her styles,
such as Crater, Horn, Bullrush and Lightning.
'Botticelli' is a leap in a different direction, and
perhaps this brooch is redolent of the wings of
the Zephyr, God of the Wind, in the Renaissance
artist's famous Birth of Venus *(1485). Maybe it's*
a riff on the oversized seashell that Venus rides
to shore, suggesting another sort of birthplace,
in this case for pearls.

Necklace, by Andrew Grima,
English, c. 1960
Freshwater pearls, topaz and 18K gold

This highly textural necklace is like confetti or
shredded cloth, in this instance with a controlled
massing of pearls brightened by topaz and gold.
Here are all the Grima strengths: choice
of materials, concept and execution.

Necklace, by Tony Duquette, American,
c. late 20th century
Blister pearls, grey cultured baroque pearls,
aquamarines and 18K gold

'Timid' was not in the Duquette design lexicon.
Everything he did – the film set for Ziegfeld
Follies, costumes for the Broadway production
of Camelot, jewelry (his first commission was for
the Duchess of Windsor), and scores of interiors
– was for the well-clad and the well-established.
Pedigree was prominent among his clients, and
so too was excess and exuberance, qualities
characteristic of all his work, including
this over-the-top hunk of a necklace. The most
recent book publication on the designer,
More is More (2009), says it all.

'Nautilus' pearl bracelet,
by Marguerite Stix, Austrian, c. 1970
Nautilus pearls, turquoise,
tortoiseshell beads and 14K gold

Marguerite Stix is best known for her shell
jewelry, though in truth she was a connoisseur
and collector of life found at the beach or sea,
including less traditional pearls. Her designs
were always fresh and clean, and always
elevated what are justly called
'gifts from the sea'.

Melo pearl bangle,
by James de Givenchy for Taffin,
American, 2007
Melo pearl, diamonds, lacquer and 18K gold

The melo pearl is one of those centre-of-
the-universe sorts of materials – its iconic
appearance demands attention. The same could
be said for James de Givenchy, a singularly
talented designer who makes modern jewelry
that is refined and luxurious.
This bangle, fitted with the rare melo
pearl, was made as a pair.

Conch pearl ring,
by René Boivin, French, c. 1960
Conch pearl, peridot,
amethyst and 18K gold

Although this is a far dressier
Boivin than those pieces dating
from the 1920s through to the 1940s,
this ring nevertheless conveys
the design thrust of the house:
a focus upon the primary material,
in this case a glorious conch pearl.

Conch pearl and wood cuff,
by Verdura, American, 2009
Conch pearls, chrysoprase, diamonds,
cocobola wood and 18K gold

For all the excess ascribed to women, they are
often frugal creatures when it comes to jewelry,
as shown here. The owner already had the stones
in another setting and never wore them, so she
turned to Verdura, who made up this wood cuff
showcasing the conch pearls. Now the cuff
is continually worn, the pearls and other
bits shine, and the owner has remade
a piece in her own style.

The House of Hemmerle

Specialist, modernist, iconoclast, purist: each word describes the Hemmerle approach to making what is currently some of the world's most exciting and unusual jewelry. Stefan Hemmerle, the head of the house whose roots go back to the Bavarian Court in the nineteenth century, is known for working with metals such as copper, brass, aluminium and silver, and pairing them with precious stones or exceptional materials. Nothing is ornate yet nothing is ordinary either. On paper, a concept drawing of Hemmerle's starfish brooch could look simple, even plain. The result astonishes. The brooch's melo pearl glows like a golden suntan. Hemmerle shuns the elaborate, preferring instead an aesthetic that links to the Bauhaus and modernism, which suits this house with its one-of-a-kind pieces. Quality trumps quantity in every case, which leads to one more adjective about the House of Hemmerle: perfectionist.

Starfish brooch, by Hemmerle, German, 2005
Melo pearl, copper and rose gold

The melo pearl is properly known as a melo melo pearl, and rather than deriving from mollusks it comes from the melo melo marine snail, whose habitat is the Indo-Pacific region. This may explain why melo pearl jewelry is more often seen in Asia; until recently it was little known in the West. All melo pearls are natural and rare, and accordingly, quite costly. Melo pearls range in colour from tan to brown, with orange – as seen here – the most desirable. Only Hemmerle would be bold enough to frame it in this copper setting.

Tassel necklace,
by Hemmerle, German, 2008
Tourmaline, sapphires, conch
pearls and copper

Here is magnificence that neither shouts nor panders: it simply is. The originality of the design is equalled by the quality of the stones and workmanship. The materials bear repeating: brown patinated copper, 373 red-pink sapphires, and in the tassel fifty-eight naturally coloured pink conch pearls.

'Lily of the Valley' brooch,
by Verdura, American, c. 1960
Cultured pearls, diamonds, emeralds,
platinum and 18K gold

*This brooch was made for the Baroness Elie
de Rothschild, whose name, Liliane, led her
to collect many lily-inspired pieces of jewelry
and objects. After making her an objet d'art
consisting of an elaborate lily of the valley
plant with her children's milk teeth, Verdura
was then commissioned by the Baroness
to make this delicate tremblant.*

'Camel' brooch, by Verdura, American, c. 1952
Baroque pearl, emeralds, cultured pearl,
seed pearls and 14K gold

*As a boy growing up at the Villa Niscemi in
Palermo, Verdura for many years led a charmed
life, complete with an amusing menagerie of
animals including baboons, rabbits, a swan,
even a marmoset with the improbable name
of Shinshitrscaramanganausaiamahowa,
otherwise known as Shin. There was also Moffo,
a camel, the inspiration for this brooch.
Moffo was eventually given to the circus
and when Verdura and his sister saw him
there years later, the designer recalled that
'He looked through us with dead eyes and
turned his head away.'*

A Verdura Creation:
The Wink of an Idea

It wasn't a doodle on a cocktail napkin, though the idea might have been just as spontaneous and imaginative: at the age of ten Nico Landrigan made a drawing of what his father, Ward Landrigan, calls 'a killer whale', complete with diamond teeth. The family was vacationing in Jamaica and young Landrigan, who now works alongside his father at the helm of the soigné Verdura, knew that some day he would make his mighty swimmer into a piece of jewelry. That sanguine certainty echoes the great Verdura himself, who mined his own childhood for shapes and figures, such as a beloved pet or the sea creatures of his native Sicily. For Nico Landrigan, that whale drawing was all but forgotten until several years ago when he asked to see some large baroque pearls. After ten months of looking at those pearls, he found himself recalling that boyhood drawing: 'once in a while you see a stone – the same way that when you lie on your back and you see an image in a cloud – and you just know. That pearl winked at me.' Although the whale had resurfaced, over a period of three years it morphed into a merry prince of a fish.

Nico Landrigan went back to one of Verdura's drawings of a fantasy fish and embarked on the long, costly process of adapting the maestro's work to an actual brooch. Something about the pearl seemed more royal than common, so a crown was added and a lion's mane ('so regal') was adapted as the golden tendrils for the fish. Were there challenges along the way? Plenty. That gradation in the fish scales, how to make them 'neither blue nor green', as Ward Landrigan mused, 'but blue-green'? Moreover, the mighty pearl had more than one smile, so which one was the dazzler? No compromises there – 'With Mother Nature, you don't impose the design. Nico adapted the brooch to the pearl.'

'Le Dauphin' brooch,
by Verdura, American, 2009
Baroque South Sea pearl, blue-green
tourmalines, diamonds, ruby,
platinum and 18K gold

In the Verdura canon, there is a limitless supply of inspiration, and this merry brooch is based on a design from 1946. However, from the time the pearl was purchased with this design in mind, it was three years in the making.

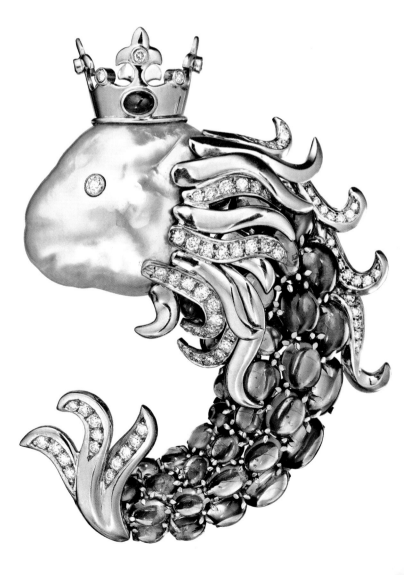

**Pair of ear pendants, by JAR, American,
c. late 20th century**
Pearls, diamonds, 18K gold and silver
*Perfection and provenance: a gifted designer,
JAR, and a talented actress, Ellen Barkin,
memorable for her role as the tough-talking
attorney in* The Big Easy *(1987).*

Why do I make jewels? Why do I want to make things never before seen?… Imagination and a notion of perfection are religion; these sacred and humble measures are the canon of making new things…. To tickle eyes, and hope, and time, this is my luxury. JAR

JAR: In Pursuit of Perfection

When considering the artistry that defines the jewelry made by JAR, born Joel Arthur Rosenthal in Brooklyn, New York, it's tempting to ignore the facts of his life and become immersed instead into the dream world that his jewelry inhabits. Indeed, JAR himself would probably say that facts of his background (an early interest in art, an education at Harvard, encouragement by jewelry expert Hans Nadelhoffer) are simply a canvas on which he has painted his life as a creator of some of the greatest jewelry ever made. When you look at JAR's steady, glorious output since he opened his atelier in the Place Vendôme in 1977, it's seductively easy to fling superlatives his way: *genius, unique, imaginative, exquisite* and, most significantly, *artist.*

In 2002, on the occasion of an exhibition of his jewelry at Somerset House, London, JAR published a door-stopper of a book: some 700 unnumbered pages, with nearly as many objects, each newly photographed for the slip-cased tome. The last page of that book has but two words, printed in silver on black: *Thank You.*

Pair of ear pendants,
by JAR, American, c. late 20th century
Pearl, seed pearls, diamonds,
18K gold and silver
This kind of beauty is never loud. It glows.

The woman who is chic is always a little different. EMILY POST

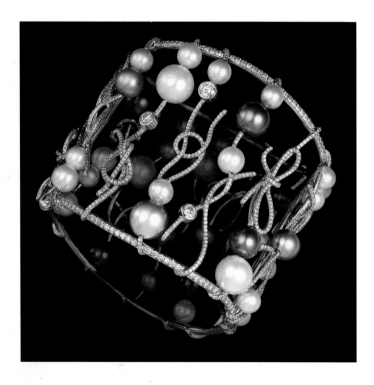

**'Jongleur' necklace, by Lorenz Bäumer,
French, 2009**
**Tahitian, Australian and freshwater pearls
with diamonds, sapphires and white gold**
*The 'Jongleur', which means juggler, displays
much of the pearl spectrum. The pearl palette
includes white, cream or ivory, pale pink and
deep pink, champagne and yellow, orange and
salmon, blue, grey, silver and black, the latter
famously scarce and hence quite valuable. There
are iridescent hues as well – pink, rosé, bronze,
green, blue or aubergine among them. It is often
the combination of the core colour and its hue
or iridescence that gives a pearl its
endless shimmer.*

**'Noeuds' bracelet, by Lorenz Bäumer,
French, 2008**
**Tahitian and freshwater pearls,
diamonds and 18K white gold**
*'Noeuds' means knots, and this delicate bracelet
is in fact composed of strings, or knots, of superb
pearls and golden ties. The name is
also an indirect reference to Bäumer's well-
known fondness for activities at sea such
as sailing and surfing.*

S

6.

Shell,
Architecture in Miniature

What do Jørn Utzon's *Sydney Opera House*, the interior of Frank Lloyd Wright's Guggenheim Museum in New York, and Santiago Calatrava's Chicago Spire have in common? They are among the many buildings that have taken the shell as inspiration. For Utzon, it was not one specific shell, but the idea of a shell covering a gastropod, for Wright it was the Japanese wonder shell (*Thatcheria mirabilis*), and for Calatrava the spiral snail shell. In her book, *The Shell: Five Hundred Million Years of Inspired Design*, Marguerite Stix describes shells as 'master builders whose architectural miracles embodied the bases of a multitude of mathematically correct vaults, arches, staircases, porticoes, and niches.'

When it comes to spiral staircases – the nautilus shell of interiors – what better way to portray cinematic madness and mayhem than in the bump-bump-thump of bodies spiralling in freefall? (Noir has always had a penchant for spiral staircases, including Hitchcock's *Notorious*, 1946, and the eponymous *The Spiral Staircase*, 1945.) As for painting and sculpture, fewer paintings are better known round the world than Botticelli's *Birth of Venus* (c. 1485), yet less well known is the shell ferrying the goddess of love to shore, probably the king or great scallop (*Pecten maximus*), though inflated by the gifted Florentine far beyond its usual dimensions of 4¾ inches (12 cm). Salvador Dalí also references the goddess in *Venus on a Shell*, his bronze sculpture of 1974; Georgia O'Keeffe set an overscaled nautilus in her beloved New Mexico hills (*Red Hills with White Shell*, 1938). Elsewhere, Edward Weston's distinctively erotic photographs of shells from the 1920s contrast with Damien Hirst's antiseptic assemblage, *Forms Without Life* (1991), a display of Thai shells in a plain glass cabinet.

Shells, you could say, are part of our cultural collective memory. Their use in Western jewelry dates to the sixteenth century, with their most significant spike in popularity occurring in the eighteenth and nineteenth centuries. And unlike with pearls, for example, or amber, anybody of any age can be a seashell collector,

One should lie empty, open, choiceless as a beach – waiting for a gift from the sea.

ANNE MORROW LINDBERGH, GIFT FROM THE SEA, 1955

for an excess of 100,000 species make shells easily admired and widely afford-able. For all the shell's ubiquitous use in jewelry, the most provocative pieces by the best jewelers retain its natural form. Armed with a shell book at your side, you could recognize coque-de-perle shells in a bracelet by Marguerite Stix; turbo earrings from Seaman Schepps, typically capped with a cabochon sap-phire, emerald or ruby; or the lion's paw in some of Verdura's dressiest jewelry. David Webb outdid even his coral beast bangles when he lined the textile cone shell with a fringe of gold and floral diamonds or sprinkled a land-snail shell with emerald flowers. In London, Andrew Grima found in the shell a perfect medium for his loving exploration of natural life; his 'Super Shells' collection from the 1970s was chic then and is today regarded as one of his greatest accomplish-ments. Interestingly, Grima, Stix, Schepps and Webb were each making jewelry with shells in the 1960s and 1970s, a period when precious stones weren't exactly démodé, but in keeping with the times were being more collegial in sharing centre stage with these organic upstarts.

Looking back to an earlier century, the shell was more adaptive, lending itself as an ideal medium for the art of cameo carving. Just as coral was a signature material of the archaeological revival, so too was the shell in the form of cameos, both predominantly from the region of Torre del Greco. By the late 1860s, the neo-classical revival included cameoists depicting the squabbling and romantically tangled Olympian gods and goddesses on brooches and magnificent parures.

The remarkable spread of shells all over the world adds to their glorious appeal, for nearly any large body of water offers armfuls of calcareous beauty. Shell-producing mollusks are surprisingly adaptable, and can be found in coral reef beds or clinging to seaweed and algae; some float on the surface of the water whereas others are deep-sea inhabitants; rivers and lakes provide haven for freshwater shells while the ocean hosts the greatest proportion. With a spin of the globe you can easily pinpoint shells in the Southwest Pacific, Mexico, the United States, Indo-Pacific, Haiti, the Galapagos Islands, the Caribbean, Madagascar, China, Japan, Australia, Indonesia, Hawaii, the Philippines and the Canary Islands. One of the first things a child is told when handed a shell is to put it up to his or her ear to discover the sound of the ocean. Nature, ever the superior teacher, is also very wise: in that moment may be born an explorer, an artist, a jeweler, but in all ways a student forever of nature's most gifted architect.

Rings, by Mesi Jilly, Austrian, 2009
Each: cowrie shell, peridot and sterling silver
*She's Austrian born, though she has since lived
in France, Italy and Chile, and somewhere along
the way got enough sand between her toes that
she became a convert to the natural beauty
and diversity of shells.*

Previous page
**Shell ear clips, by David Webb,
American, 1964–65**
Shells, coral, turquoise and 18K gold
*Shell ear clips were a staple of the Duchess of
Windsor's jewelry box. From left: checkered
nerite (Nerita tesselleta), capped with gold and
turquoise; yellow with brown and white stripe
Cuban tree snails (Polymita picta) with gold
lozenges; orange, brown and white stripe Cuban
tree snails (Polymita picta) with gold lozenges;
and white with brown stripe Cuban tree snails
(Polymita picta) with gold lozenges*

Cameo brooch, c. 19th century

Shell and gold

*Around the time this brooch was made, a young
woman reading was a subject that appealed to
painters and artists, with noteworthy paintings
by Mary Cassatt, Pierre Renoir and, most
similar to this brooch, Winslow Homer's
The New Novel of 1877.*

**Shell cameo earrings,
probably Italian, c. 1840
Shell and gold**

*The interest in Greek mythology fuelled many
decorations on shell cameo jewelry, in this case
those nearly doomed lovers, Cupid and Psyche.*

Cameo necklace,
French and Italian, c. 1830s
Conch shell and gold

The conch, a gastropod, was often used in
Europe for cameo carving – the periostracum,
or outer layer, was smoothed away to reveal the
white middle layer, which was carved against the
darker background of the innermost layer.

Opposite
Shell necklace and five brooches,
Italian, c. mid-19th century
Shells and gold

The six large shell cameos represent major
Greek and Roman deities. From top centre,
clockwise: Apollo, Minerva, Diana, Bacchante,
Juno and Mars. The small cameos are assorted
dancing figures. Among the five brooches, the
two large profiles are each Minerva. At centre
is Aurora, the Roman goddess of dawn, in her
chariot, and to her left is Neptune,
god of the sea.

Mad for Mythology

If you were one of the moneyed travellers of the early to middle years of the nineteenth century, you were going to places fashionably of interest. You were also, as the saying goes, 'getting culture', and what better way to improve your learning than through the classics. Italy and Greece, the twin foundations of Roman and Greek civilization, were 'must' destinations. The archaeological revival was producing an abundance of coral and lava jewelry, but it was in shell cameo work that figures could be depicted in relief with greater dimensionality; the contrast of the carved white inner layer against the dark shell ground yielded a clarity that anticipated the effects of black-and-white portrait photography. The shells intended for the carver's hand were often imported from Africa and the West Indies, and were used to portray some of the better-known and more powerful gods and goddesses on Mount Olympus, who symbolized everything from fertility to famine; day to night; leadership to banishment; and of course, love to war. Popular figures from the period included a sprinkling of Greeks and Romans: Zeus/Jupiter, Hera/Juno, Athena/Minerva, Artemis/Diana, Aphrodite/Venus and Ares/Mars. With a cluster of shell cameos, the bejeweled lady of this time could be a walking encyclopedia of story and myth.

Gods and Goddesses of the Classical Revival

Apollo—the god of medicine, healing and also the plague; typically shown with a snake.

Bacchante—one of the female followers of Bacchus, the god of wine, often depicted dancing in the forest.

Diana—the chaste hunter and Roman twin sister of Apollo; has a quiver of arrows at her side and often a hunting dog.

Juno—the mother of Mars and Apollo, patron goddess of Rome and protector of women in marriage and childbirth; often shown with a peacock.

Mars—Roman god of war, typically portrayed in full battle regalia such as a helmet and shield.

Minerva—Goddess associated with wisdom, poetry and music; often depicted with a rooster.

Venus—the goddess of love and beauty.

Zeus—the Great One, all-powerful ruler of Mount Olympus.

The Artful Butterfly

Here are two examples of shell jewelry using the Australian clam brooch (*Neotrigonia margaritacea*), a deep-water shell found in southern Australia. It's amusing that one natural material is used to suggest another form in nature, the always-appealing butterfly, an especially popular motif around this time.

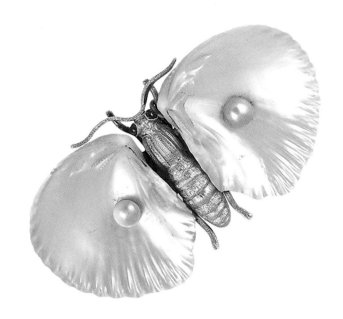

My pleasures are the most intense known to man: writing and butterfly hunting. VLADIMIR NABOKOV

Above

Butterfly brooch, c. 1870
Clam shells, pearls, rubies and gold

Butterfly brooch, c. 1870
Clam shells, pearls, emeralds and gold

France and the Gallic Cockerel

The association of the rooster with France derives from a bit of amusing word play. In Latin, *gallus* means both rooster and a resident of Gaul, hence the rooster as emblematic of Gallic France. In the Middle Ages, roosters were shown on bell towers, more for their cock-a-doodle-doo than any political swagger, though by the time of the French Revolution the cock was proudly displayed on the French flag. In 1830, the cock replaced the fleur-de-lis as the national emblem, in 1848 it was added to the seal of the Republic, and from 1899 to 1914 it was featured on the 20-franc coin. Lalique's depiction of a cockerel in his art (he made a belt buckle similar to the brooch, also around this time) could be viewed as a statement of national pride.

Art Nouveau cockerel brooch,
by René Lalique, French, c. 1900
Shell, pearl and 18K gold
As metaphor, as an example of working with natural forms, and as pure wit and genius, Lalique's cockerel brooch famously succeeds. The artist has depicted two roosters engaged in a duel over the pearl, which is naturally adhered to the centre of the shell; yet this is not a fight to the finish, but an existential struggle for something that neither will ever have.

Bracelet, by Mellerio dits Meller,
French, c. 1960s
Abalone shell, diamonds and 18K gold

*Originally from the Lombardy region of Italy, the
Mellerios came to Paris in the early seventeenth
century and by 1613 had set up business. Within
a couple of decades they had become the royal
jewelers to King Louis XIII, who granted them the
right to adapt their surname into French, hence
they became Mellerio dits Meller. The firm was
also the first jeweler to set up shop in 1815 on
the rue de la Paix, where it remains today,
fourteen generations later.*

Brooch, by Mellerio dits Meller,
French, c. 1960s
Abalone shell, diamonds and 18K gold

*This dazzling brooch and bracelet may have
been made by twelfth- or thirteenth-generation
Mellerios; but regardless which branch of
the family tree was involved, the set shows
a deep appreciation for the blazing colours
of the abalone shell (Haliotis sp.).*

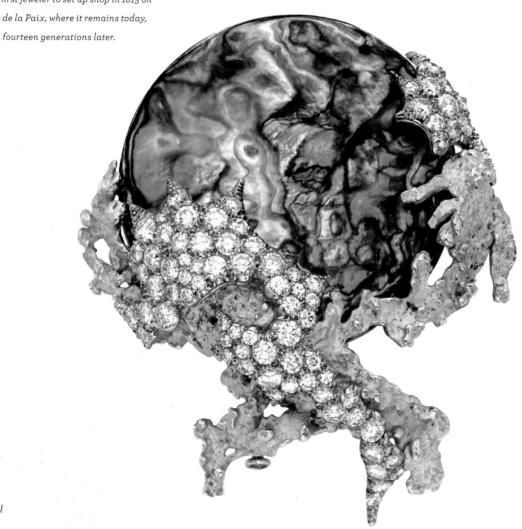

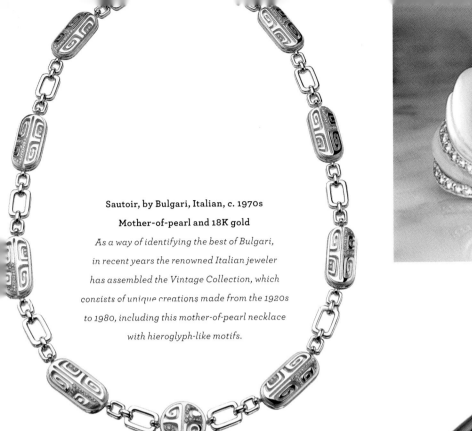

Sautoir, by Bulgari, Italian, c. 1970s
Mother-of-pearl and 18K gold

As a way of identifying the best of Bulgari,
in recent years the renowned Italian jeweler
has assembled the Vintage Collection, which
consists of unique creations made from the 1920s
to 1980, including this mother-of-pearl necklace
with hieroglyph-like motifs.

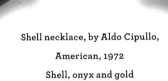

Above right
Pair of ear clips, by Mauboussin, French, c. 1970
Mother-of-pearl, diamonds and 18K gold

In business since 1827, Mauboussin Joaillerie
(originally Noury) made a fashionable splash
with its Art Deco jewelry at the Paris Expo
of 1925. From that point forward, Georges
Mauboussin combined fine jewelry skills with
savvy business ideas, such as marketing theme
shows based on precious stones. He also had
high-profile clients, including Hollywood
actresses Marlene Dietrich and Greta Garbo,
and worldly royals such as Queen Nazli of Egypt.
Also of note is the house's strong showing with
retro jewelry of the 1950s–70s.

Shell necklace, by Aldo Cipullo,
American, 1972
Shell, onyx and gold

Cartier designer Aldo Cipullo created the iconic
'Love Bracelet' for the house in 1969. That all-
gold band – a 'golden handcuff' – was meant to
symbolize loyalty: a special screwdriver was
used to bolt the hinged parts, making them a
unified whole. Cartier sold it to famous couples
such as Elizabeth Taylor and Richard Burton,
Sophia Loren and Carlo Ponti. This expensive
expression of togetherness was followed up with
such other witty creations as the 'Love Noose',
the nail ring, and countless other smart designs.
Cipullo, who died young at the age of forty-two
in 1984, received the Coty American Fashion
Critics Award for Jewelry in 1974.

Marguerite Stix, the Artful Translator of Shells

'As a gifted child, a prize-winning art student, a concentration-camp survivor, a penniless refugee, a designer of accessories for the haute couture, a factory worker, a recognized sculptor and painter, a creator of widely sought-after jewelry and of fantastic ephemera, she never departed from her deeply felt celebration of life and its meaning.' This is taken from the only book about Marguerite Stix, who was born in Vienna and travelled a long road – literally and figuratively – over the course of her sixty-eight years. Apart from this monograph, however, not enough has been said about Marguerite Stix, except by those knowing insiders who speak her name with reverence and esteem her pioneering spirit and gift for understatement. Where David Webb, for example, made High Art with shells, or Seaman Schepps made Costly Jewelry with shells, Stix was content to make the shells *art*, never mind a quota of diamonds or emeralds. Her own fascination with shells was lifelong, but once she and her husband, Hugh Stix, decided to collaborate on a shells book, her interest soared. In 1964, the Stixes turned their Greenwich Village home into a salon to show off their outstanding collection of shells gathered worldwide to a group that included writers, artists and the high society crowd. Not long after, shells were 'in', and so was Marguerite. It was unexpected fanfare.

From there, drawings of shells and playful assemblages of shells led to baby steps in making jewelry with shells. A fortuitous pairing of artist and medium had begun: dappled cone shells turned into rings bound in enamel and gold; turritellas, turbos and tree snails dangled as pendant necklaces; abalone and mother-of-pearl shimmered as bracelets braced by a gold netting; the nautilus became a purse; a lion's paw was wisely reserved for decisive, statement-making pieces. With shells, Marguerite wrote that she 'wanted to direct attention to a world of ideas that might give fresh meaning and stimulation to the contemporary arts – to free-form creation....' In her case, grasp and reach were evenly matched.

Shell rings, by Marguerite Stix,
Austrian, c. 1970
Left: Cone shell, red enamel and 18K gold
Right: Cone shell, green enamel and 18K gold
The Marguerite Stix shell ring became what art critic Richard McLanathan described as a 'symbol of elegance, as recognizable as an autograph'. The owner of these rings was herself the epitome of elegance and propriety, American actress Dina Merrill. Her family pedigree included some of the country's best-known names: her father was the financier Edward F. Hutton and her mother Marjorie Merriweather Post. The glacial beauty grew up in Mar-a-Lago, the famous Palm Beach pile that had 114 rooms and cost nearly eight million dollars when it was built in 1927. The cone shell used in both rings comes from the Indo-Pacific region: the marble cone, Conus marmoreus, *is perhaps used in the red enamel ring, whereas the* Conus striatus *is used in the green enamel setting.*

Opposite below right
Shell bracelet, by Marguerite Stix,
Austrian, c. 1970
Shells, lapis lazuli, blue zircons and 14K gold
Marguerite Stix was a sculptor before she came to working with shells and that sense of dimensionality shows up in this bracelet, a gold 'cage' that fits around the wrist.

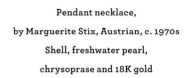

Above

'Margaretacea' shell ring,

by Marguerite Stix, Austrian, c. 1965

Shell and 14K gold

In an act of humour and sly nod to the scientific nomenclature of shells, Stix has named this design after herself. And why not, for the 'Margaretacea' is the artist's signature piece. A bivalve, perhaps the pink tellin, is cleverly used to frame the ring front, all of it framed in gold, which further accentuates the natural shell hinge.

Below

Pair of ear pendants, by Marguerite Stix, American, c. late 1960s–early 1970s

Shells, sapphires and gold

This beautifully coloured shell is aptly named the strawberry top shell (Clanculus puniceus), a gastropod and member of the Trochidae family. Marguerite Stix was first a collector of shells, and no doubt this was among the many that she and her husband collected when researching their book on shells published in 1972.

Pendant necklace,

by Marguerite Stix, Austrian, c. 1970s

Shell, freshwater pearl,

chrysoprase and 18K gold

The lion's paw (Lyropecten nodosa) was among the shells the artist used for her most dramatic necklaces, where it was often encased in gold and allowed to swing, pendant style, from a chain. Here the artist has made a textured gold-hinged box of two lion's paw shells suspended by a single then double chain. Both inventive though simple – like all of Stix's work – the chain has been alternately strung with polished gold rods and freshwater pearls; a chrysoprase cabochon, joined to the chain, suspends a chrysoprase pendant drop, making this necklace in effect a double pendant.

We have tried to let the shells speak for themselves, in their own language. MARGUERITE STIX

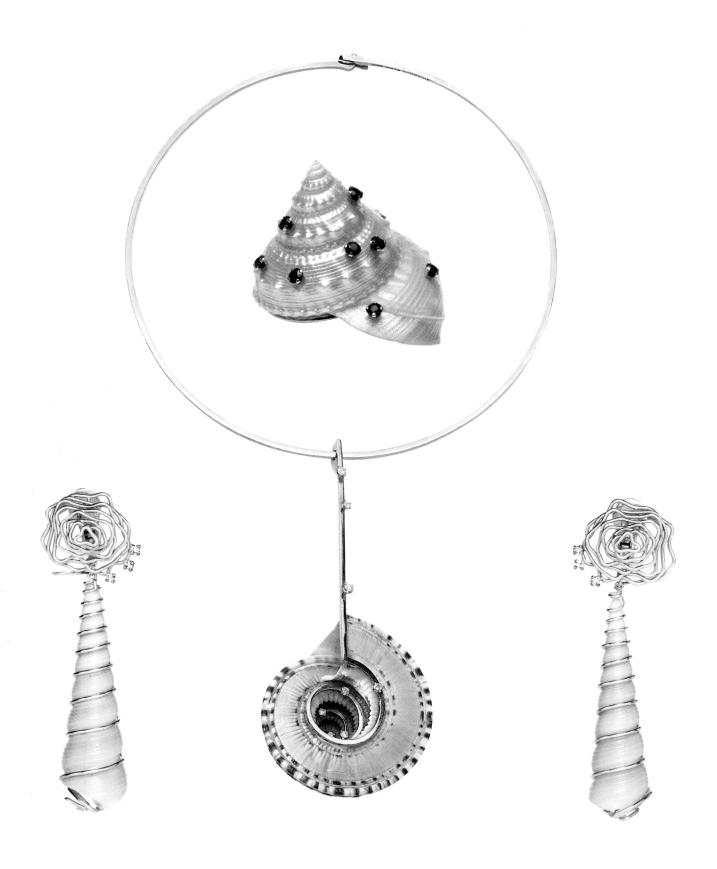

Andrew Grima, the Flamboyant Gentleman Jeweler of Jermyn Street

Sea urchins morphed into mushrooms, ammonite fossils became ram's horns, black Tahitian pearls turned into ducks riding crested waves of amethyst crystals – what couldn't Andrew Grima do? The organic world was his métier and muse, and in Grima's creative hands jewelry was shown as never before: wild, unfettered and wonderfully original, showcasing textured gold settings with unconventional stones and natural materials. Just as critics talk about a new voice in fiction, Grima was that new voice in the jewelry world of the 1960s and 1970s. As he often remarked, he began designing when precious stones were the main prop for brooches and rings, the subject matter equally predictable. But London wasn't simply changing, it was the centre of change – the Beatles, Mary Quant and the miniskirt, Twiggy, Vidal Sassoon, to name but a few of the newly hip, were the cultural tempest into which Grima so artfully blended.

Consider some accomplishments: for Princess Margaret he cast Scottish lichen into a gold brooch; he once made a gold brooch based on pencil shavings; and he designed eighty unique watches with semi-precious stones for Omega in 1971 for his 'About Time' collection, which he described as 'seeing time through stones'. He liked to group his work by themes, and some of the most beloved – though hard to find today – works from the 1960s and 1970s are 'Rock Revival', uncut semi-precious stones and minerals (1969); 'About Time' (1971); 'Super Shells' (1975); and 'Sticks and Stones', uncut tourmalines and semi-precious stones set in gold and platinum (1977).

He was the gentleman jeweler of Jermyn Street (nearly every photo shows him smoking a pipe), where his shop, designed by his two brothers, was an architectural coup of natural materials and forms, and was officially opened by Lord Snowdon. Grima was among the first to blend Art with High Society: he drove an Aston Martin and loved sea shells; fell into designing jewelry by happenstance and was granted the Royal Warrant as jeweler by appointment to the Queen; and counted as his loyal flock of customers Ursula Andress, Jackie Onassis and the Queen. It should come as no surprise, then, that one of his ancestors helped to make the Trevi fountain in Rome.

'Super Shell' brooch,
by Andrew Grima, English, 1972
Shell, rubies and gold

Andrew Grima may have chosen the shell for this
lustrous brooch because of the amount of nacre
– it's called a trochidae (Bathybembix crumpii),
a gastropod found mainly in the Sea of Japan.

'Super Shell' necklace,
by Andrew Grima, English, 1972
Shell, diamonds and 18K gold

That phrase, Super Shell, is so seventies and
so perfect: at what other time in the twentieth
century could you get away with using the word
'super' to name a collection of fine jewelry?

'Super Shell' ear clips,
by Andrew Grima, English, 1972
Spiral shells, diamonds and gold

The slender elongated shell duplicate turritella
(Turritella duplicata) *is ideal for adding a bit*
of weight and swing to these ear pendants.
The gold wire and diamond surmounts spiral
around the shell body, forming a magnificent
scaffolding in gold.

'The Lichen Suite',
by Gilbert Albert, Swiss, c. 1970
Shells, pink, yellow and grey cultured pearls,
diamonds and 18K gold

Gilbert Albert is among Switzerland's most
celebrated jewelers – his work has been shown
in such venues as the important modern jewelry
exhibition in 1961 at London's Goldsmiths' Hall;
the Gulbenkian Museum in Lisbon; and he was
the first living artist invited to show his work at
the Kremlin, in 1991. Though the word 'typical'
could never apply to Albert, 'The Lichen Suite'
features distinctive signs of his buoyant spirit,
which embraces such natural materials as shells
(in this case, the spider conch shell, Lambis sp.),
and cultured pearls mixed with diamonds,
also beloved by the designer.

Opposite above
Brooch, by Verdura, American, c. 2009
Lion's paw shell, diamonds and 18K gold
Marguerite Stix was a great collector of shells,
and when she died Verdura bought some of
the shells from her estate, including the ever-
distinguished lion's paw shell (Lyropecten
nodosus), shown here with striking diamond
rivulets. The fan-shaped bivalve, also known
as the Atlantic lion's paw, ranges from the
southeastern United States to Brazil.

Verdura, the Shell Man of Palermo

Nature was Fulco di Verdura's favourite store. There he did his best shopping, returning time and again for pansies, forget-me-nots and lilies of the valley; animals that he tamed with loving charm such as dogs and cats, swans and storks, hippos, elephants and camels; fruit that was both tempting and delicious – ripe strawberries, exotic pineapples and pomegranates – and trees bearing maple leaves, pinecones and acorns. If he had one significant purchase, however, that topped all others, it would have to be shells. Over a period of many years beginning in the 1930s,

scallops, turbos, quahogs, tree snails, conchs, clamshells and the ever-mesmerizing nautilus were each magically transformed by Verdura and made even more beautiful when glittering with precious stones or massed with pearls. And the shell that commanded centre stage for Verdura was the regal lion's paw shell, *Lyropecten nodosus*.

The colour wheel for this nobly-shaped shell is like a hairdresser's dream, from blond to brown and all the stops in between: platinum blond, sunny, California blond, strawberry blond, deep red and brunette. Verdura made the most of the redhead, beginning in circa 1930 when he dressed it in reams of diamonds and sapphires, the dark navy hues in rich contrast to the red and white, giving it a nautical look that his friend Chanel might have admired. For the strawberry blond shell, the look was softer and prettier, a gentle blend of citrines and diamonds. More recently the look is clean and modern, with a stream of diamonds washing over the ribs of the shell. Perhaps it's more than coincidence that the jeweler who did so much with shells was born in Conca d'Oro, the Golden Conch, of Palermo.

Brooch, by Cartier, French, c. 1960

Lion's paw shell, sapphires,

turquoise and 18K gold

The colouration is deeply beautiful, with the combined heat from the play of the sapphires and turquoise. The surprising point about this brooch is its maker – one doesn't normally associate Cartier with shell jewelry.

Pair of ear clips,

by Verdura, American, c. 1940

Cone shell, coral and 18K gold

Linnaeus designated this shell Conus ebraeus *in
1758, though today it is also known as the Hebrew
cone shell. It's a reef dweller, often found just
burrowed beneath a thin layer of sand in parts of
the Galapagos, Central America and Australia.
To Verdura, however, its variable spots against
a white ground might have suggested both sea
and animal (the leopard, perhaps), or maybe it
was simply a shell whose fabulous graphic marks
allowed him to spin his own magic.*

Brooch and matching ear clips,

by Verdura, American, c. 1940

White nacre turban shells, coral and 18K gold

*Is it a four-pointed star, a variation on the
Maltese Cross (of which Verdura made many),
or does it simply reflect the delight of invention?
There is nothing arbitrary about the gold wire
wrapping on the brooch – on closer inspection
it is a beautiful nautical knot, which, as any
sailor knows, is always the masterful pairing
of form and function.*

Shell cufflinks, Italian,

c. 1990s

Shell and gold

Collection Camilla Dietz Bergeron Ltd.
The beauty of cufflinks, especially today,
is that they truly are a 'one size fits all'
– men and women.

Shell earrings, by Renato Cipullo,

American, 2008

Turbo shell, rubies and sapphires

An affinity for design runs in the Cipullo
family, as seen in this pair of earrings
by Renato, Aldo's brother.

Shell cufflinks,

by Marguerite Stix, Austrian, 1965

Shell and gold

Collection Francesca Romana Davis.
This white bivalve is a ubiquitous player
in the Stix canon, appearing in rings,
bracelets, and cufflinks.

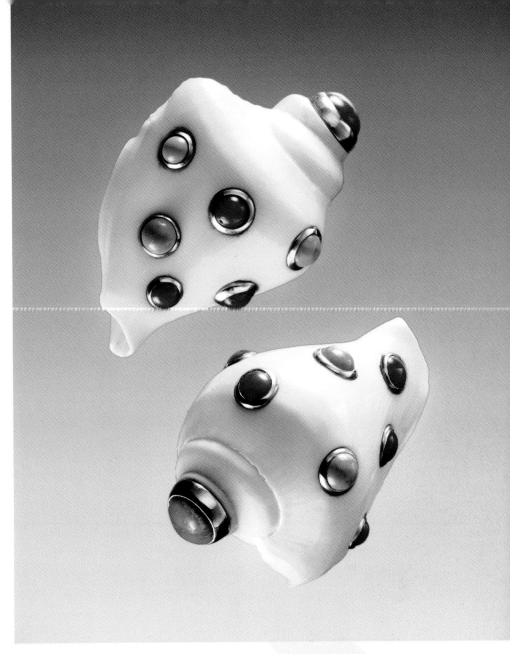

Sorting Out Shells

The shell world is vast and complex, beginning with the field of study itself. For example, are you a conchologist or a malacologist? The former studies shells, whereas the latter focuses on the study of mollusks. For the beginner interested in learning about what shells are used in jewelry, you can dip your toe into both waters...

Mollusk—The largest marine phylum with roughly 100,000 species, second only to arthropods; dates back to the Cambrian period, 550,000 million years ago. The mollusk is an invertebrate and typically has a muscular head and a foot used for locomotion, which attaches itself to its underwater lair, and a non-muscular mass that inhabits the calcareous shell. The distinctive hard shell protects the soft body. There are freshwater, marine and land species, such as land snails. Sizes range from the very small (less than 1mm in diameter) to the aptly named giant clam (4 feet or 1.2 metres wide and weighing as much as 500 pounds or 225 kg). There are seven classes of mollusks, though only four appear in shell jewelry: *gastropods, bivalves, cephalopods* and, to a much lesser degree, *scaphopoda.*

Men's dress set, by Trianon, 1985
Cuban tree snail shells, lapis lazuli
and 18K yellow gold
What makes this dress set special is not just the smart combination of shell and lapis, but the spectacular chromatic yellow of the Cuban tree snail shell (Polymita picta). Among its land-snail fauna, Cuba has more than 1,000 species endemic to the Oriente province, where the tree snail makes its home. Each shell is unique, making it a challenge for the determined jeweler of this gentleman's dress set. The tree snail shell always coils clockwise, and is also known as the painted helix.

Gastropods—From the Greek meaning 'stomach foot'. These are univalves, thus having one shell. They have eyes and motor along on one foot only. The shell is *equiangular*. Includes the abalone, conch, cowrie, helmut, whelk and top or trochus shells. The only class that has adapted to living on land. Used for most cameo jewelry. Includes approximately 40,000 marine species, and 25,000 freshwater and land species.

Equiangular or logarithmic spiral—Discovered by René Descartes (1596–1650). Refers to the growth spiral or *spiral mirabilis*: as the spiral grows in a geometric progression it retains its shape. The nautilus is the classic example of equiangular growth.

Bivalves—The second largest class of mollusks. They have neither head nor eyes. Common examples of this hinged shell are clams, scallops, razor shells, mussels and oysters. The distinctive lion's paw was a favourite used by Marguerite Stix and Verdura. Includes more than 15,000 species.

Cephalopods—The ancient class of mollusks dating back to the late Cambrian period, some 570 to 510 million years ago. The most intelligent of the mollusks. Includes the chambered nautilus (*Nautilus pompilius*), one of the best-recognized species in the shell world, as well as the less well-known sub-class of octopus, squid and cuttlefish. Andrew Grima used the nautilus in his 'Super Shells' collection. Includes approximately 1,000 species.

Scaphopoda—Marine dwellers known as tusk or tooth shells. A small class of some 350 species.

Men's dress set, by Antora, Italian, 2009
Shells and 18K yellow gold

The zigzag or zebra nerite shell (Neritina Communis) *has about fifty different species, and though the shell is not rare its colouration is fanciful and appealing. Most species are found in mangroves in the Philippines and other parts of the western Pacific.*

T

7.

Tortoiseshell,
Marbling Most Appetizing

'Manina' hand
brooch, by Nardi,
Italian, c. 1960

What is it about admiring tortoiseshell that gives you an appetite? If you've ever cooked with chocolate or done much baking, then you know how your mouth waters and your heart tugs when chocolate is poured into a vanilla-coloured batter, the two entering into a dance of sorts as the chocolate forms swirls and whorls before it is blended into the golden mixture. Tortoiseshell produces a similar effect: the rich nuances of colour – the caramels, the chocolate browns, the honey and espresso tones – are what confer the sumptuousness of the best tortoiseshell jewelry.

For this natural beauty we should thank the hawksbill turtle, *Eretmochelys imbricata*, resident of tropical waters and lover of sandy beaches. Although justifiably protected as an endangered species today, hundreds of years ago this marine turtle was fished not for food (that's the green turtle, *Chelonia mydas*, from whom terrapin soup is long famed), but for its horny plates, or scutes. The deeper tortoiseshell tones come from the scutes along the carapace, whereas the blond colouration is from the scutes that cover the belly. The hawksbill, so named because its tapered head resembles a bird's beak, has made its home along the coastlines of the Atlantic, Pacific and Indian Oceans, dining mostly on certain sponges among coral reef communities, though being an omnivore it also enjoys a meal of mollusks, crustaceans, fish and some marine algae. Under the best circumstances, the hawksbill can live to be fifty years old, although the biological clock for females doesn't kick in until they're at least twenty years of age, nearly halfway through their life span.

In the Western world, goods made from tortoiseshell first made their mark in the seventeenth century, particularly in France where tortoiseshell was applied as a veneer or as marquetry for fine furniture, though it was mainly in England during the early years of the nineteenth century that the craft of working with tortoiseshell flourished. The nature-loving Victorians adapted floral and celestial motifs onto many hand goods at the time, including jewelry. Tortoiseshell was ideal in this regard, for as a thermoplastic it could be heated and thus shaped into hair ornaments decorative and functional, jewelry, lockets, boxes and fans. In a few exceptional cases, cameo reliefs – miniatures of classical motifs or a beloved – were sculpted in tortoiseshell, such as the elegant beribboned suite of necklace and earrings with a cameo on the pendant and earrings, at right, or on the magnificent cuffs and matching earrings possibly made by the American jewelers Caldwell, in the mid-1800s, opposite. When adding gold or silver, the old French technique of piqué was employed. Taking advantage of tortoiseshell's malleability, piqué was essentially a technique for applying decorative inlay, from the simplest design such as straight lines encircling a bangle to more ornate patterns such as floral cornucopias.

Notwithstanding tortoiseshell's natural beauty and workable qualities, its popularity in England among Queen Victoria's loyal subjects surged when it was deemed acceptable jewelry for half-mourning. The Queen, who famously imposed a long period of mourning on her kingdom after her husband died (she remained in mourning for the rest of her life), relented that after full mourning, from six months to a year, ladies could switch from dark jet jewelry to something lighter, with a bit of lift. Thus tortoiseshell, along with niello and gunmetal, came to be worn by women of all stations.

As with many luxury goods, mass production and imitation tortoiseshell eventually entered the marketplace and by the end of the nineteenth century most quality tortoiseshell jewelry was rarely seen. But leave it to the French, for whom beauty is never bound by time, rules or fads, to create perhaps the most regal example of tortoiseshell: a comb head that seems to spread its arms in welcome, a sort of *Winged Victory*, regal with pearls and diamonds, a runway example of elegance created at a time when one century was ending and a new one, the modern century, was just beginning.

The tortoise is very fond of water, drinking large quantities, and wallowing in the mud.

CHARLES DARWIN, THE VOYAGE OF THE BEAGLE, 1839

Page 157

**'Manina' hand brooch, by Nardi,
Italian, c. 1960**

Tortoiseshell and multi-gems

*The Venetian firm of Nardi is best known for its
carved ebony moretti, or blackamoors, based on
the Moor of Venice in Shakespeare's 'Othello'.
The manina, which means small hand, is another
familiar Nardi motif, and is a bejeweled play on
the small wooden hand used to count candidates
during the election of the doge under the
Republic of Venice (7th century AD–1797).*

Opposite

**Cameo pendant necklace
and ear pendants, c. 19th century**

Tortoiseshell

*A marvellously intact suite. The pendant
is actually two pendants: the carved ribbon and
the locket, with a head shown in relief.*

**Pair of cameo cuffs and matching earrings,
possibly by J. E. Caldwell,
American, c. 1860–80**

Tortoiseshell

*The probable maker of these cuffs,
J. E. Caldwell & Co., was the Philadelphia firm
of James Emmett Caldwell (1831–81). Caldwell
was born in Poughkeepsie, New York, and
apprenticed both in New York and Philadelphia
before opening his own shop in the 1830s with a
partner, James M. Bennett. Given the propensity
to memorialize one's family, the figures on
the cuffs may be the parents of the children
portrayed on the earrings.*

Chain and locket, American, c. 1870

Tortoiseshell

*The beautifully carved monogram on the
locket would have been done for the lady who
owned this piece. Tortoiseshell, like jet, was
considered a suitable material for mourning,
and this locket may have contained some
memento of a deceased family member
or close friend.*

Tortoiseshell brooch,

English, c. 1850

Tortoiseshell and gold

*The tortoiseshell was steamed in order
to form this buckle strap brooch, signifying
the British Order of the Garter, whose strictly
limited membership always included the
monarch, at this time, Queen Victoria.*

Opposite

Art Nouveau winged comb head,

French, c. 1900

Tortoiseshell, pearls, diamonds,

gold and silver

*More dyed blond than brunette,
the tortoiseshell for this comb was in fact
bleached so that it took on a veneer of
transparency, which accounts for the way
it seems to glow from within. When first made,
the winged comb was set as a tiara comb.*

Bracquemond and Vitta: Artist and Patron

For struggling artists working on the perimeter of success, a moneyed patron can seem like manna from heaven, relief from worry and compromise. When a real bond is forged, works of great art result, as was the case in the collaboration between Félix Bracquemond and the Baron Vitta in late nineteenth-century Paris. By then Bracquemond was well along in life, having spent much of it as an engraver and painter. He was also at home in the Paris milieu of artists and writers, counting Degas, Rodin, Millet and Edmond de Goncourt among them. The baron lived well and with pride – his apartment at 51 Avenue des Champs Elysées was ideal for showing off his collection of Art Nouveau. (He also maintained a well-appointed villa on Lake Geneva.) Baron Vitta was an important collector, and as a patron he used his wealth and desire for perfection to positive effect. In Bracquemond he found a shared passion for beauty. The exceptional hair combs, shown here, were among the various objects Baron Vitta commissioned from Bracquemond. For both the baron and Bracquemond, beauty or 'art' was meant to trump utility, at all cost.

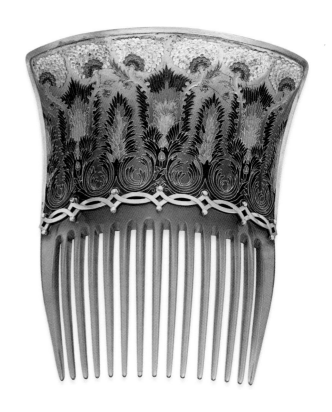

Pair of Art Nouveau hair combs,
by Félix Bracquemond and Alexandre Riquet,
French, 1900
Tortoiseshell, plique-à-jour enamel
and 18K yellow and rose gold
Each comb is an arched panel with a flared top elaborately decorated with vibrant, multi-coloured plique-à-jour enamel flowers and foliate scrolling detail against the plique-à-jour enamel background of chartreuse or pink (bold colour choices at any time). And at 5¼ by 5½ inches (13.3 by 14 cm), the scale of these combs is massive, especially considering that they were to be worn as a pair. This particular toilet, made for the Baron Vitta, originally included a handmade mirror, inset with a gold medallion by Rodin, a friend of Bracquemond's.

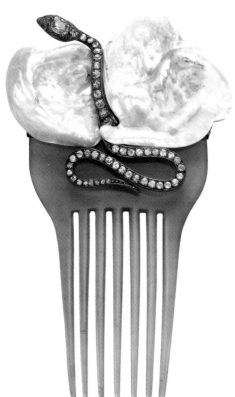

Hair comb, American, c. early 20th century
Tortoiseshell and rhinestones
Painted rhinestones add a bit of fanciness
and sparkle to this quietly pretty comb.

Hair comb, American, c. 19th century
Tortoiseshell
Luscious loops of tortoiseshell – the classic
Art Nouveau whiplash – would have perfectly
echoed the hairstyles of the period, with swags
of piled-up hair, chignons set loose and high,
and a ringlet sprig on the forehead or nape
of the neck de rigueur.

Art Nouveau serpent hair comb, by Charles
Boutet de Monvel, French, 1890–1910
Tortoiseshell, mother-of-pearl,
peridots and silver
Serpents have long been a familiar jewelry
motif, though the apogee of snakedom was in
the mid-1800s, when it seemed these slithering
creatures were nearly ubiquitous.

Piqué ear pendants, American?, c. 1880

Tortoiseshell and gold

Below right

Ear pendants, c. 1940s

Tortoiseshell

What goes around comes around: though
modern, the concentric hoops here echo those
from a hundred years earlier.

Grapevine piqué bangle, American?, c. 1880

Tortoiseshell and gold

Piqué, A Touch of Class

Technically there is more than one kind of piqué, just as there was more than one artisan engaged in refining the process in more than one country. A Neapolitan by the name of Laurentini introduced the technique in the seventeenth century, although the esteemed French cabinet maker André-Charles Boulle is regarded as the person who raised piqué to an art. (Indeed, Boulle was so skilled at marquetry that an anglicized version of his name references his style, known as 'buhl' work.) From France the use of piqué spread to England, Germany and Holland, though it is chiefly in England where piqué and tortoiseshell jewelry are most commonly allied. Tortoiseshell is a natural thermoplastic, making it ideal for piqué work, which in essence entails the insertion of gold or silver rods into warmed tortoiseshell to create patterns from the simple to the sublime. For *piqué point*, thin wires were pushed through the heated tortoiseshell and then filed flush with the surface; as the tortoiseshell cooled, it formed a tight grip or seal around the metal inlay. More elaborate designs, such as the scalloped earrings with the rounded triangular design, circa 1860s, opposite, were the result of *piqué posé*; here an outline motif in fine wire was pressed into the warmed tortoiseshell and then allowed to cool. But whether it was *point* or *posé*, piqué was an ideal inlay for making decorative patterns in the forgiving medium of tortoiseshell, lending to the piece a touch of classy ornamentation.

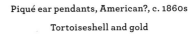

Piqué ear pendants, American?, c. 1860s
Tortoiseshell and gold

Stars and Greek key piqué ear pendants,
American?, c. 1880
Tortoiseshell and gold
The Greek key design harkened back to a
time when neoclassical motifs were in vogue,
appearing on everything from architecture
to home furnishings, textiles and jewelry.

A Repertoire of Design in Piqué

To look at tortoiseshell creations in jewelry from the mid- to-late 1800s is to discover a visual index of Victorian interests. The best tortoiseshell piqué jewelry dates from the middle of the century, when the work was done by hand; at that time the fondness for nature shows up on many pieces – grapevines curl around bangles, cornucopias burst from the centre of brooches, flowers such as roses blossom on swags and Creole-style ovals. Popular interest in science and astronomy was growing, and though planets don't appear on jewelry, stars do, in wonderful clusters and of all sizes, from nearly regimental alignments to all-over patterns. Birds and butterflies give form to tortoiseshell brooches, again with sophisticated piqué work of dazzling design. By 1870, manufacturers in Birmingham had learned how to mass-produce piqué-style tortoiseshell jewelry, by which time simpler geometric forms appear, including Greek keys, hearts, trefoils, dots and bands of gold or silver.

Horse bangle, c. 1950s
Tortoiseshell, ivory, diamonds and gold

Tortoiseshell box, by David Webb,
American, 1964
Tortoiseshell body, diamonds,
emeralds and 18K gold

Although Webb used seashells for his earrings,
he was typically content to mimic nature. This
piece, however, is hardly standard in his canon.
Here the entire turtle shell forms the cover of this
jewel-coated box that is more in keeping with
the nineteenth century than the later twentieth
century. But perhaps it was done as a special
commission. And perhaps this little turtle
fetched up in someone's garden, already more
dead than alive – or so one can only hope.

8.

Wood,
Simple Perfection

*a*fter food and water, wood is perhaps the one living, organic material whose existence has been most nurturing to our own over the millennia. From wood we get shelter, fuel for cooking and warmth. But the ABCs of wood go much further than these basic needs. Wood appears in niches both large and small in our lives: consider musical instruments such as violins and guitars; sports equipment such as tennis rackets, skis, golf clubs, baseball and cricket bats; salad bowls and spoons, toothpicks and chopsticks; wagons, sleds, cars (the famous American Woody Wagon of the 1940s), boats, even gondolas. But it's when thinking about wood and the arts that the finer application of wood comes to mind, such as engraving and printmaking, sculpture (Renaissance Madonnas, Native American Indian totem poles, tribal art), and carving (from Grinling Gibbons to Louise Nevelson). As for fine furniture, that is a story rich in examples from countries worldwide, including the work of the Englishman Thomas Chippendale, the Frenchman Emile-Jacques Ruhlmann and the American Duncan Phyfe.

It is this gentle slide from function to adornment and decoration where wood quietly moves into the jeweler's realm. Just as wood is entrenched in our lives, so examples of its use in fine jewelry can be found over the past 150 years, much of it anything but ordinary. To make an object of beauty with pearls is a little like putting make-up on a naturally attractive woman – you can't go wrong. But with wood the challenge is taking this raw and inherently utilitarian material and making of it something that stands out, not loudly as with diamonds, but quietly, subtly, almost modestly. Wood does not beg for centre stage or star billing. Its presence alone gives it gravitas and merits our attention.

Examples of its resilient beauty abound. Mention Cartier and you might think of precious gems or platinum, but in 1930 Cartier made a wedding box out of a burl wood for a pair of newlyweds, making it surely one of the more stylish gifts from wood a young married couple might receive. There is of course the

Autumn leaves tiara,
by Tim Gosling
for David Linley,
English, 2001

great René Boivin, whose near reverence for wood resulted in rings and cuffs fashioned from ebony and sandalwood that are exemplars of refined simplicity. Artist Alexander Calder, a magician with wire, was also a hobby dabbler in jewelry making and in his use of wood.

One of the great surprises in wood jewelry is the little-known French designer Catherine Noll. Among works that date primarily from the 1970s and 1980s, she made more than four dozen rings, each winning exercises in geometry and excursions into working with many kinds of wood. Like balancing a plate on a stick, these are rings that at first sight might appear to topple over, victims of misalignment or proportion. But there are no faux pas here, for Noll understands plumb weight and uses that knowledge adroitly.

In contrast to Noll's select fan base, there is Seaman Schepps, the New York jeweler whose cunning bijoux adorned Park Avenue and Hollywood. The Schepps name is known for many things, especially for working elegant wonders in wood. His simple gold and wood link bracelets, first made in the 1940s, are enduring classics. Using a variety of wood, such as ebony, rosewood, walnut and sandalwood, Schepps's wood link bracelets became a staple for the well-dressed woman and remain so, decades later. A different kind of classic was produced by William Spratling, a highly-educated American who fell in love with the dusty Mexican town of Taxco, where he lived and produced jewelry for nearly two decades. Working with ebony and silver, for example, Spratling's jewelry quickly transcended local notoriety and through such connections as his college room-mate, William Faulkner, writers, artists and actors began buying his ebony and silver cuffs, pins and rings.

Among contemporary and studio designers, wood is used in ways that surprise, amuse, impress and are environmentally correct. Christine Brandt, Noma Copley, Liv Blåvarp, Kiff Slemmons and Anthony Roussel are each creating something utterly 'new' with wood, which is remarkable for a material whose origins in jewelry date back to 1500 BC.

Who has not heard of Whitby jet and admired its unsurpassable lustre, with which it is a compliment to compare a beautiful woman's eyes?

HARPER'S NEW MONTHLY MAGAZINE, 1884

Whitby jet and three-stone diamond ring, English, 1880–1900
Whitby jet, diamonds and gold
Like amber, jet is both lightweight and when rubbed becomes electrically charged. That static electricity gave rise to the ancient belief that jet could ward off the devil and dissolve spells.

Jet and Whitby: The Beginning of a Beautiful Friendship

There is nothing new about jet: it's 135 million years old and derives from the fossilized wood of a single species, the monkey tree (*Araucaria*). Though it occurs in various parts of the world, historians and experts all agree that the best jet for making jewelry comes from Whitby in Yorkshire, on the northeastern coast of England. If you were looking for jet, you'd head straight to the shale cliffs between Robin Hood's Bay and Boulby. One jet hunter (as men in the trade were traditionally known) took a pragmatic view of the trade: 'It's just like puttin' thy hond in a lott'ry. Yo' may soon lose a lot, an' soon gain a lot.' But 'gain a lot' Whitby did, for although the relationship between Whitby and jet began quietly – just one shop sold the jewelry in 1808–10 – within a few decades Whitby had become *the* source for the London fashion crowd seeking jet jewelry.

Its heyday came about when Queen Victoria switched to jet jewelry as part of her mourning attire upon the death in 1861 of her husband, Prince Albert. (Were a lady to be introduced at court, she was expected to wear jet with her similarly sombre clothing.) In time, jet was no longer just for those in mourning, but also to signify friendship, love and betrothal. Happiness and sadness, it would seem, are never really that far apart, in life or in art.

Whitby jet brooch. English, c. 1880
Hand-carved Whitby jet
This brooch is a triumph in patriotism and unity: the hand-carved rose, shamrock and thistle represent England, Ireland and Scotland.

The Many Varieties of Wood

African Ebony (*Diospyros crassiflora*)—Nearly all black but with some grey streaks; used by René Boivin in some timepieces and domed rings.

Beechwood—Beige to medium brown of medium density.

Boxwood (*Casearia praecox*)—Camel brown in colour and dense. Also known as West Indian or Venezuelan boxwood.

Brazilian Cherry (*Hymenaea courbaril*)— Reddish brown with a deep lustre, this hardwood, also known as jatoba and courbaril, is from the South American tropical rainforest. Admired for its use in fine furniture, architectural details and parquet.

Cocobolo, Mexican Rosewood (*Dalbergia retusa*)—A beautiful and dramatic rosewood with a deep orange-brown hue.

Ebony, Macassar (*Diospyros celebica*)—This hard black wood has other colouration such as grey and near-reds.

Guadua (*Guadua angustifolia*)—A tropical bamboo well suited for use in architectural and design projects; the tree is particularly effective at removing carbon dioxide from the air.

Lacewood—Also known as silky oak; medium to light brown.

Lignum vitae—Also known as ironwood; the hardest wood in the world.

Maple (*Acer* family)—Also known as a tonewood because it carries sound waves effectively and thus is used in the production of musical instruments.

Maple Burl—Originates along the west coast of North America; the telltale signs of this burl are the masses of bark inclusions.

Padauk (*Pterocarpus soyauxii*)—From South Africa; bright orange.

Palisander (*Dalbergia nigra*)—Also known as Brazilian Rosewood, the genus Dalbergia, which is native to tropical regions in Central and South America, Africa, Madagascar and Asia. A hardwood that is dark with an exotic pattern; highly prized for making furniture, it was used by the great Art Deco furniture designer J. Rual and in the 1950s by Herman Miller and Charles and Ray Eames.

Purpleheart (*Leguminosae* family)—Also known as amaranth, violetwood, tananeo and sake; from Central and South America. When cut the wood is a bright purple that darkens over time; used for marquetry and inlay.

Rosewood (genus *Dalbergia*)—Any number of varieties of timber; in addition to the cocobolo it includes African blackwood, kingwood and tulipwood.

Queensland Leichhardt (*Nauclea orientalis*)—Also known as yellow cheesewood or cheesewood; found in the eastern and northern woodlands of Australia as well as the tropical rainforests of the northeast.

Snakewood (*Piratinera guianensis*)—Originates in Surinam, South America. One of the hardest woods, thus making it very difficult to work with; also has a tendency to crack unless skilfully handled. So-named because its markings resemble snakeskin, though sometimes called letterwood in England (these same markings are comparable to hieroglyphics); other names include *amourette*, leopard wood, speckled wood. Used by Van Cleef & Arpels for their wood clematis and butterfly pins.

Zebrawood (*Leguminosae* family; *Microberlinia brazzavillensis*)—An exotic wood distinguished by its zebra-like alternating light and dark markings, most commonly found in West Africa.

Zitan (*Pterocarpus*)—A member of the rosewood family, from southern Chinese provinces as well as Southeast Asia. This exceptionally hard wood – so dense that it sinks in water – is also slow growing, reaching only around 30 feet (10 metres) in three hundred years. Its nearly purple-black colour destined its use initially only for the Imperial household during the Ming Dynasty (1368–1644), after which time it became rare due to excessive lumbering. It remains scarce and thus costly.

**Clematis brooch, by Van Cleef & Arpels,
French, c. 1970s
Wood, diamonds and 18K gold**

*The French call it amourette, we call it
snakewood or letterwood, and it is surely one
of the world's most exquisite and rare woods.
The interest in combining exotic wood with
gold first shows up in the early years of the
twentieth century in the Van Cleef & Arpels
repertoire, and returns variously – in the 1950s,
early 1970s and again in 2000. Clearly, this is a
relationship intended to last, and the clematis
in wood is one of the more distinctive designs
of this famous house.*

**Beetle brooch, by Fabrice, French, c. 1990
Exotic hardwood**

*Several times the size of the real thing, and yet,
thankfully, more art than science.*

The Boivin Heart:
Ceci N'est Pas Une Pipe

This is not a heart. It is a piece of sculpture, a statement, a work in perfect architectural balance and proportion. To understand Boivin is to understand several people at once – René Boivin himself, born 1864 but short-lived; his wife, Jeanne Poiret, sister to the famous couturier Paul Poiret, who took over the jewelry business upon his death; Suzanne Belperron, who started as a young salesgirl at the boutique in 1921 and in the decade she spent there designed spectacular pieces, though unsigned; her successor, Juliette Moutarde, the longest keeper of the flame, outlasting Madame Boivin by nearly a dozen years; and Boivin's youngest daughter, Germaine, who also designed for the house. Therefore it is the House of Boivin one honours, and rightfully so. Madame Boivin made a virtue (and reputation) of working with materials from the natural world around her – she collected leaves and bark, shell and rock, which inspired her many fluid forms, especially her use of wood.

Heart pendant,
by René Boivin, French, c. 1960
Wood and 18K gold
The addition of the gold beads gives
a suggestion of decoration to this
smartly large heart pendant.

Wood and gold bangle,
by Boivin, French, c. 1980
Wood and gold
The piece is modern, but the sensibility
is still on clean design that spotlights
the inherent beauty of the wood.

Wedding box, by Cartier, French, c. April 1930
Burl wood (possibly black walnut), 18K gold,
sterling silver and sapphire cabochon

Imagine the lucky couple receiving this
Cartier box as a wedding gift! Telltale signs
of their life and interests are here: cards
(aces only, of course), wine, cigarettes, music,
the darling rabbit as cupid, and of course
the bride and groom. The meaning of the
lettering on the right of the box is a mystery.
Nor do we know the answer to the question:
'Are you in a good humour?'

Wristwatch, Van Cleef & Arpels, French, 1932
Wood, enamel and leather cord

This is wood watch #35741, 'Bracelet montre',
according to the vast Van Cleef & Arpels archives
in Paris. There it was painted in gouache on
small lined cardstock on 14 January 1932.

William Spratling, The American Father of Mexican Silver

William Spratling first went to Mexico in 1926 to deliver a lecture on architecture, and by 1929 he had become so enchanted with Taxco, then a neglected silver mining town some 75 miles southwest of Mexico City, that he moved there. Working with hundreds of artisans in his studio, Spratling designed jewelry based on pre-Cortes Aztec and Olmec motifs using ancient techniques, thus spawning a renaissance in Mexico's silver-making tradition.

Don't make it prettier. Always keep it simple.

WILLIAM SPRATLING

Necklace, by William Spratling,
American, c. 1940–46
Rosewood and sterling silver
Spratling was a bon vivant with an abundance of talent and interests. One of his closest friends was his former college roommate, the writer William Faulkner; he once taught architecture at Tulane University; he helped to make Taxco a destination spot for celebrities such as Bette Davis, Clare Boothe Luce and Errol Flynn; he had his own private zoo (including an ocelot, macaws and a boa constrictor); at one time he owned seven Siamese cats and twenty-three Great Danes; he was a sailor, a small plane pilot, and once travelled to Europe on a zeppelin.

'Pyramid' bracelet, by William Spratling,
American, c. 1940s
Ebony and sterling silver
Mayan pyramids may have been the inspiration for this bracelet and others like it. During the 1940s, Spratling made the pyramid shape in other materials including bronze, copper and sterling silver, though most of these are less than ½ inch (0.65 cm) deep, whereas this cuff, at 1¼ inches (3.2 cm), is a significant statement piece of jewelry.

Double 'G' Stands for Gucci Goods

Well before terms such as 'branding' entered the zeitgeist, to those who knew Gucci in the 1960s the name conjured up telltale icons. There was the ubiquitous red and green striped webbing, inspired by the saddle girth, that appeared on men's loafers, women's handbags (surprisingly, women seemed indifferent whether the stripe matched the rest of their outfit), even luggage and belts. Then there was the horse bit or snaffle, that defining piece of hardware used as a closure on wallets and as ornament on loafers. (The Gucci loafer was, and still is, *the* sign of nonchalant class, worn by the classiest of hoofers, Fred Astaire, and in the 1960s became part of the permanent collection of the Costume Institute at the Metropolitan Museum of Art, New York.) The monogram 'G' was also introduced in the 1960s, and like Italian espresso, you could have a single or a double on your purse or travel gear. Also long-lasting was the hobo bag, first called the 'Constance' and then renamed the 'Jackie O', after it was carried by that eponymous arbiter of chic. But another handbag also defined the Florentine house, and that one displayed a bamboo handle. Wood was used with élan on other objects from the venerable Florentine company, such as watches and in combination with silver. In the 1950s and 1960s Gucci rode a wave of style that burnishes this period as its classic best.

Buckle bracelet, by Gucci, Italian, c. 1960s
Wood and sterling silver
Produced at the height of Gucci's fame, this buckle bracelet borrows from menswear and also reinforces, however subliminally, the house's popular association with clasps, toggles, buckles and other hardware.

Circle wristwatch,
by Gucci, Italian, c. 1960–70s
Wood and 18K gold
By today's standards of the Gucci 'look', this watch seems decidedly un-flashy, though in fact it was in keeping with other wood watches from the same period. The hardware fasteners are part of the toggle, snaffle and other Gucci insignia.

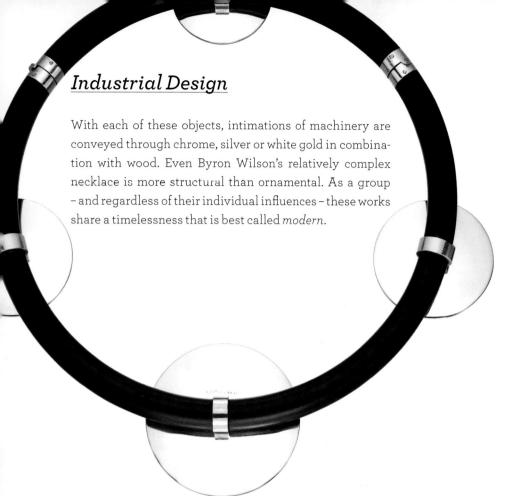

Industrial Design

With each of these objects, intimations of machinery are conveyed through chrome, silver or white gold in combination with wood. Even Byron Wilson's relatively complex necklace is more structural than ornamental. As a group – and regardless of their individual influences – these works share a timelessness that is best called *modern*.

Art Deco necklace and bangle,
by Jean Fouquet, French, c. 1931
Polished ebony, chrome and 18K gold

By the time this set was made, the Parisian avant-garde had embraced Surrealism and was being influenced by such faraway tribal cultures as Papua New Guinea and Africa. Fouquet was among those attracted to tribal-influenced jewelry, as exemplified by the ebony and chrome disks. A telling local influence was Nancy Cunard, the 1920s socialite whose trademark look included an armful of large bangles.

The Radical Chic of Jean Fouquet

Jewelry and gold pieces must be works of art while also responding to the same needs as industrial objects.

JEAN FOUQUET,
JEWELRY AND GOLD, 1931

The Fouquet name was for many years associated with some of the finest jewelry made in France, from the early 1800s until 1936, when the shop was shuttered. The youngest Fouquet to join the firm was Jean, who in 1919 began work alongside his talented father, Georges. But whereas Fouquet *père* straddled Art Nouveau and Art Deco with success, Fouquet *fils* was dedicated to the Modern Movement, largely inspired by the famous Paris Expo of 1925. Jean Fouquet, like his contemporaries Gérard Sandoz and Jean Després, was an exemplar of that new breed of jeweler known as the *bijoutier-artiste*, or artist-jeweler. The emphasis was not on precious gemstones but on inherent beauty, less on curves and decoration and more on geometry and Machine Age qualities. Excess was banished; economy of design was exalted. Chrome or silver was the new gold, Cubism was in, and Paris – because of people like Jean Fouquet – proved once again that it was the leader worldwide in jewelry.

**Necklace, designed by Amalia del Ponte
for GEM Montebello, Italian, 1969
White gold, ebony and ivory**

*Del Ponte was born in Milan, where she studied
and began making art. Although she's known as
a sculptor, she also made striking jewelry that
excelled at unusual combinations of materials
and forms. Her approach is both playful and
purposeful: to employ materials as agents of
provocation. GEM Montebello was a short-lived
Milanese company (1967–78) that commissioned
limited-edition jewelry from more than fifty
artists, among them Man Ray, Ettore Sottsass,
Niki de Saint Phalle, Alex Katz,
Sonia Delaunay and Hans Richter.*

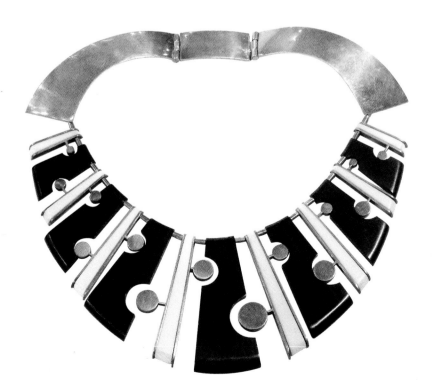

**Necklace, by Byron Wilson,
American, 1952
Silver, ebony and ivory**

*Wilson was among the earliest members of the
Metal Arts Guild in the San Francisco Bay Area,
founded in 1951 as a way of unifying the studio
jewelry community of Northern California.
Wilson used dental tools to fabricate some of his
pieces, and was one of the first American jewelers
to experiment with combinations of silver, wood,
bone and ivory. More bib than necklace, this
piece is a successful feat of engineering.*

Wood and ivory ring,

by Catherine Noll, French, c. 1975

Macasser ebony and ivory

*Looking at this ring is like looking through
the 'wrong' end of a telescope: turn it around
and you are seeing a table by Catherine Noll's
grandfather. Yet this was no mistake, but instead
the talented forward motion of one artist
learning from another, who just
so happened to be family.*

Wood and ivory ring,

by Catherine Noll, French, c. 1975

Spalted maple (?) and ivory

*When Catherine Noll took over her grandfather's
atelier outside Paris, she also inherited his
inventory of exotic woods, which she beautifully
shaped into rings, necklaces, cuffs and the
occasional pair of earrings.*

Wood and resin ring,

by Catherine Noll, French, c. 1976

Exotic wood and resin

*Among the scores of rings that she designed,
Noll made frequent use of resin.*

Catherine Noll: A Natural Woodworker

Once upon a time in the early 1970s a talented young Frenchwoman set to working with wood. She had inherited both her talent and studio from her grandfather, Alexandre Noll, a gifted maker of wood furniture in the 1940s and 1950s. Typically she set wood and ivory, one into or atop the other, resulting in objects that were rings, but if they had been made significantly larger might have been dining tables or side tables, rather like those made by her grandfather. It just so happened they were jewelry. Occasionally she teamed caramel-hued resins with wood for rings, moulded Lucite with ivory into stylish cuffs or plied Lucite into thick disks to create weirdly oblong pendant necklaces. As for the necklaces, stylistically they ranged from ethnic to Gallic, as much tribal as they were Eileen Gray. Tragically, Catherine Noll died at the age of forty-seven in 1992, also the year her work was included in the third jewelry biennial at the Musée des Arts Décoratifs in Paris.

Wood and ivory necklace,
by Catherine Noll, French, c. 1975
Ebony and ivory

In addition to making her own wood-based
jewelry, Catherine Noll also designed jewelry for
Nina Ricci, Chanel, Baccarat and Christian Dior.

Wood and ivory earrings,
by Catherine Noll, French, c. 1976
Ebony and ivory

A Passion for Butterflies

Paris and Tokyo are sister cities, and their most recent alliance by way of Van Cleef & Arpels is both auspicious and spectacular. In early 2000, the jewelry firm embarked on a collaboration with Hakose San, a master lacquer artisan, to create butterfly brooches using snakewood and lacquer. In his Wajima workshop, Hakose San interpreted traditional Japanese motifs and patterns using the ancient lacquer technique known as *Kodai-ji makie*. In all, seventeen designs were created, each in a limited edition of thirty, every one of them made by hand and with exceptional materials. The 'Papillon' collection was formally released to the public in 2006. The four pieces shown here are the first, second, third and thirteenth in the series of seventeen.

'Hana Karakusa' butterfly brooch,
by Van Cleef & Arpels, French, c. 2000
Snakewood, yellow gold, lacquer, diamonds,
pink and blue mother-of-pearl, quail eggshell;
first in a limited edition of seventeen
This breathtaking brooch is made using
the traditional Japanese Kodai-ji makie
decorative lacquer technique, which dates to
the Moyomama period, in the sixteenth century,
when it was first created for the Kodai-ji Temple
in Kyoto. Makie, or 'sprinkled picture', involves
sprinkling gold or silver powder over a lacquered
surface, onto which a design is then made. Here,
hana karakusa refers to flowers (hana) shown in
an arabesque pattern (karakusa).

'Kikumakie' butterfly brooch,
by Van Cleef & Arpels, French, 2004
Gold, wood, diamonds, lacquer, pink and blue
pearls; second in a limited edition of seventeen
Kiku means chrysanthemum, one of the most
frequently depicted flowers in Japanese art.
The fragrant chrysanthemum symbolizes purity
and aristocracy, and was also a 'fountain of
youth' – one could extend one life's just by
drinking the dew on the flower!

'Shinobu' butterfly brooch,
by Van Cleef & Arpels, French, c. 2006
Snakewood, yellow gold, lacquer and
diamonds; third in a limited
edition of seventeen

The shinobu *or fern leaf is a typical Japanese
motif used for centuries, although the patterning
of the leaves differs between craftsmen.
The deep gold tones on this brooch are
a result of twenty different gold powders
of varying brilliancy.*

'Ryusui' butterfly brooch,
by Van Cleef & Arpels, French, 2008
Snakewood, yellow gold, silver, diamonds
and lacquer; thirteenth in a limited
edition of seventeen

The highly graphic ryusui *design is meant
to depict running water and is inspired by
the art of Japan's mid-Edo period, in the
eighteenth century.*

Bangle, by JAR, American, c. 1985
Ebony, chalcedony, amethyst and diamonds
Even the most disparate-seeming pieces by
JAR announce the hand of an artist: each is
individual yet unified by remarkable conception
and execution.

Bangle, by Hemmerle, German, 2005
Amaranth wood, sapphires, white gold
and black-finished silver
Just as a luxury car drives soundlessly,
so too this bangle glides on the arm,
with the hush of quiet beauty.

The Elegants: 'Loveliness Extreme'

Each of these designers takes great pride in their work, each has a strikingly individual style, and each is exceptional. What further unites them is the consistent path they've chosen: elegance, at any price. Although Gertrude Stein's line 'a rose is a rose is a rose' is often (mis)quoted, it is the second line in her poem 'Sacred Emily' of 1913 that is most apt about these designers: 'Loveliness extreme.'

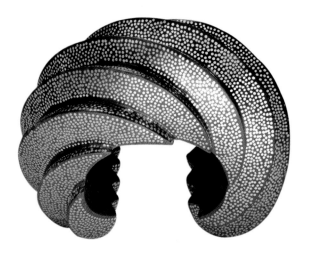

'Kinsky' wood cuff,
by Patricia Von Musulin, American, 1990
Hand-carved lignum vitae wood
and sterling silver inlay
Lignum vitae, literally 'the wood of life', is so
hard that it's often used to make mallet heads.
Here it's used for this classic motif of Patricia
Von Musulin's work – a swirl-like design, which is
all the more impressive considering the density
of this wood. So too are the inlays of silver,
akin to nineteenth-century piqué work often
done in tortoiseshell. If the cuff looks familiar,
it's because it was worn in ivory by a young
German star in the now-famous Avedon portrait,
'Nastassja Kinsky and the Serpent', of 1981.

'Diamond Tree' brooch, by James de Givenchy
for Sotheby's Diamonds, American, 2006
Palisander **wood and diamonds**

Some might say it's in the blood, this penchant
for design and pursuit of excellence, in the man
whose uncle was beloved couturier Hubert de
Givenchy. But matters of nature or nurture aside,
James de Givenchy distinguished himself with
a flair for beauty rendered with the cool eye of
a modernist, and in 1996 opened his business
under the one-word name Taffin. In partnership
with Sotheby's Diamonds, in 2006 he launched
a limited-edition collection of fifteen pieces that
showcased exquisite and unusual diamonds
with equally exquisite and unusual materials.
One of those remarkable pieces is this tree
brooch – the form is nearly stark but not so the
leaves, nourished, as it were, by their diamond
illumination. Here is the ultimate in living jewelry.

'Honey Life' ear pendants,
by Wallace Chan, Chinese, 2008
Zitan **wood, spinels, pink crystals and coral**

Though he is perhaps best known for devising
new ways in working with titanium, Wallace
Chan finds some of his greatest inspiration in
nature in such organic materials as wood and
coral. Zitan, rare in China and an exotic wood
of great density, is suited to Chan's penchant
for dramatic pieces. As he says, 'Nature
conceives. I complete.'

'The Tilda Necklace', by Alexis Bittar,
American, c. 2008
Teak wood, coral beads and
gold pyramid beads
*Why Tilda? For designer Alexis Bittar, the
actress-performance artist Tilda Swinton
'stands for real strength and individuality',*

*which is understatement made with a knowing
smile. After all, this is the woman who became
a one-woman artwork at London's Serpentine
Gallery in 1995 when she spent seven days on
display in a glass container asleep, or pretending
to be. This one-of-a-kind necklace is an
homage to originality.*

Bean necklace, by Elsa Peretti
for Tiffany & Co., Italian, 2008
Wood and gold lacquer
*This softly curved biomorphic form suggests
everything from the foetal position and
beginning of life to the legume, a cornerstone
of nutrition.*

Elsa Peretti: Tiffany's Working Girl

This is the woman who said 'I design for the working girl' when she was hired in 1974 by Tiffany yet who was also a favourite model of Helmut Newton, Scavullo and Halston, with whom she co-designed some pieces. She was born in Italy, studied in Switzerland, and worked in Barcelona before settling in New York. Certainly not your average working girl, and yet the simplicity of her pieces, the reliance on organic form, the introduction of silver, and the conviction that jewelry should be affordable have made a name for Peretti and introduced a signature style recognized everywhere.

Lopsided hearts, the snake, the apple, the starfish, 'diamonds by the yard', the smooth cuff, the mesh necklace, and, above all, her 'lucky bean', are all Peretti-isms, for which she has been awarded such coveted prizes as the Coty in 1971 and Accessory Designer of the Year by the CFDA in 1996. In 1977, *Newsweek* magazine's cover story, 'Jewelry's New Dazzle', pronounced that jewelry as the new accessory 'began with the arrival of a tempestuous Italian ex-model named Elsa Peretti'. To which, one could add, this tempest in a Tiffany teapot has created a lasting brew.

Life, people and nature. My ideas begin with a simple element like a stone or a piece of driftwood. ELSA PERETTI

The fish has been around for thousands and thousands of years. It's a natural creature, very fluid. It's a continuous form, and it survives. And it's not contrived.

FRANK GEHRY

'Fish' pendant, by Frank Gehry for Tiffany & Co., American, 2006
Ebony and silver
The shape is spare yet unmistakably a fish, and the slight wave of the inset silver describes its aquatic habitat – a rendering of simple reduction.

Frank Gehry, Big Fish Architect

When Tiffany & Company brought in architect Frank Gehry in 2009 as their featured designer, they landed a very big fish. One of the most celebrated and well-known American architects of the post-World War II period, Gehry has received accolades from around the world, including being named a Pritzker Prize laureate in 1989. This is the man who has said that there are no rules, and who asked rhetorically at one point, 'How wiggly can you get and still make a building?' Questions the jewelry world might ask are, 'How do you get the architect of Bilbao, the Vitra Design Museum and the Walt Disney Concert Hall, among his hundreds of important buildings, to reduce the scale of his creations to the size of a woman's wrist? How does a man who thinks about windows consider earlobes?'

Gehry's response has been work that is surprisingly delicate: his crumpled-paper ring in gold, starfish in black titanium, or torque bangle in agate are each simple and expressive. Given the architect's appreciation for music, there is in fact a lyrical lightness to his work for Tiffany, not unlike the rhythms of his built work.

As for fish, since he was a boy, Gehry has regarded the aquatic dweller as a symbol for life, tellingly expressed in 1987 when he built the Fishdance Restaurant in Kobe, Japan, and in his Tiffany fish pendant, necklaces and bracelets in ebony, rutilated quartz and jade.

Kara Ross, Knowing What Women Want

For Kara Ross, her crystal ball into the future was a tourmaline. This young designer has been in the public eye as a jewelry designer since 2002, but this belies a formative fact: at the age of thirteen while on a family trip in Africa her parents allowed her to purchase a stone as a souvenir. It was a tourmaline, and once home in Philadelphia, Kara Ross went a step further: she designed a ring for herself. It even had diamonds. This wasn't the usual dream-meets-destiny saga of a teenager, though it did show a path for success – a gift for design, pluck and dedication. These days Kara Ross works with natural materials such as exotic and common woods (even jet, popular in the later nineteenth century, comes into play), or less familiar stones such as black coral or green rutilated quartz, and gives them a fashionable twist: it's a high-meets-low feat, and it works. The constant throughout is a modernist eye for geometry and scale (these are not pieces for the shy or the insecure), made by a woman who appears to know what other women want.

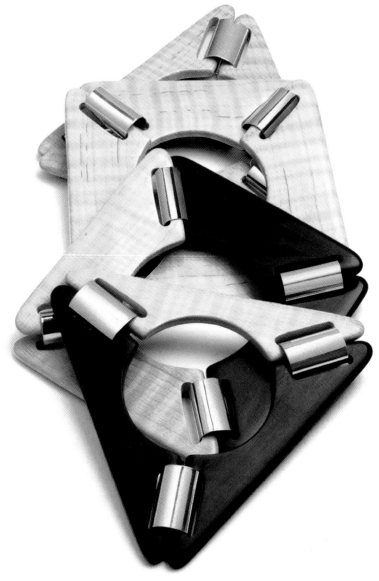

Square and triangular bangles,
by Kara Ross, American, 2007
Maple, ebony and 18K gold

Pair of ear pendants,
by Kara Ross, American, 2009
Ebony, black diamonds and 18K gold
Black diamonds, technically called carbonado (Portuguese for burned), confound even the best scientists as to their origin. A recent theory is that they emerged from dying stars, and may be some four billion years old.

> *I, for a long time, tried to transform the everyday, the common objects that are taken for granted, into poetry to wear.*
>
> NOMA COPLEY

Noma Copley, Elevating the Everyday

Noma Copley spent a lifetime making art and jewelry that was a send-up of the everyday elevated by an insistence on fine materials. A gold safety pin became a necklace (a deuce were pierced earrings), sterling silver and ivory were shaped into a bar of Ivory soap and worn as a ring, a pencil became as flexible as a noodle and turned into a bangle. This tension between humour and high-end is what provides the élan when you see a pair of soft drink bottle caps, for instance, turned into eighteen-carat gold cuff links.

She was born early in the twentieth century in Minneapolis, and by the 1950s had married William Copley, who was friends with artists such as Man Ray and Max Ernst, and who collected their work and others by well-regarded Surrealists and Dadaists. By 1967, Noma Copley began making jewelry, and in less than ten years her work was being shown in New York. She was, and still is, underknown. Yet her witty creations – and there were plenty (her 'kisses by the inch', gold *x*'s strung on a thin chain, is brilliant) – are now collectors' items. Which is pretty good for an unsung American Dadaist.

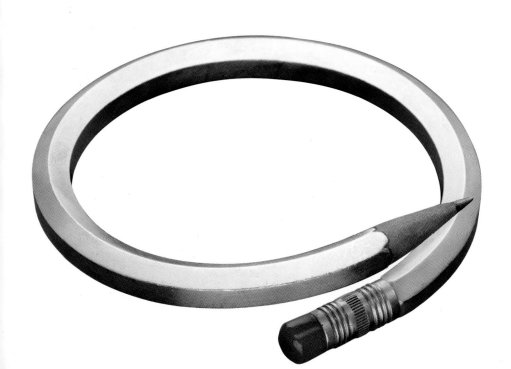

'Bent Pencil' bangle, by Noma Copley,
American, c. 1999
Wood, coral, steel, 22K and 18K gold
Dada meets the everyday in the world of Noma Copley. The artist made seven or eight of these bracelets, deliberately leaving blank the place where the manufacturer's name would be so that the owner could engrave her or his own name.

Pencil necklace, by Lee Hale, American, 2003
Eberhard Faber Blackwing 602 pencils
and hematite beads

Lee Hale's grandmother used the Blackwing pencil to keep score during bridge games; when her grandmother died, the artist inherited her stash but sacrificed just one Blackwing – seen here – for a pencil necklace, which Hale says unapologetically 'is not for sale'.

Pencil necklace, by Lee Hale, 1998
Derwent Studio pencils and onyx beads

Not just any pencil will do – paper-wrapped pencils, for example, will shred and certain painted pencils peel. Flat pencils, triangular pencils (those from Britain's Tate Galleries, for example), coloured pencils, and pencils with funny logos or names are the best candidates.

Ode to the Eberhard Faber Blackwing 602: 'Half the Pressure, Twice the Speed'

Writers, editors, draughtsmen and artists have for decades been the members-at-large of a dedicated group: they all revere the Eberhard Faber Blackwing 602. The body was graphite grey, the lead a soft 4B, and the eraser legendary *and* unique. The ruddy pink eraser was rectangular, not round, and thus fit into a rectangular ferrule, held in place with a slim aluminium clip. In repose and in action, it was what one journalist called 'the DeLorean Gullwing Coupe of the pencil world'. No matter what you were writing or drawing, with the Blackwing in hand you felt confident, prepared, ready to wage battle with the blank page. Or at least that's how such greats as John Steinbeck, Stephen Sondheim, Truman Capote and Tom Wolfe felt when they were making literary history.

All this private luxury went asunder when in the 1990s the only machine in the world that could manufacture the ferrule broke, the inventory was used up, and then the little metal clip that held the ferrule was gone too. So it's 'bye bye birdie', though nowadays you can score a Blackwing 602 on eBay for thirty dollars each, up from the fifty cents or dollar it cost in the 1980s. Sadly, the inimitable wood-cased pencil, with its never smudgy black lead, is in Pencil Heaven. All that remains is its endearing slogan, now epitaph, *Half the Pressure, Twice the Speed.*

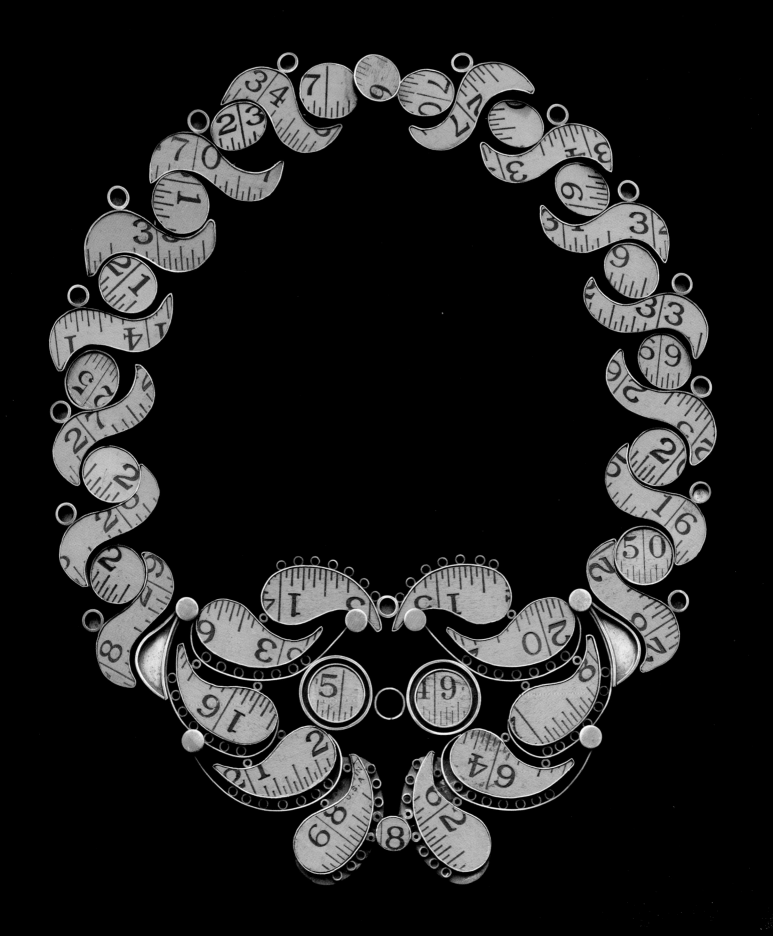

Kiff Slemmons, Challenging Perfection and Completion

As the daughter of a newspaper publisher and editor, Kiff Slemmons comes naturally to pencils and wood, rulers, typewriter keys and other tools of the trade. Some of her work focuses on found objects, on reusing what is discarded, not for the sake of frugality but in an effort to explore transformation and adaptation. (Having come of age during the Vietnam War, Slemmons brings a social conscience to the chipped and the abandoned.) Rather than strive for unblemished perfection, Kiff Slemmons wants the viewer to witness change, to be aware of cracks and fissures, to understand 'repair' as an idea and as 'living history' rather than as something to be covered up. Investigation is part of the artist's process, and she makes us look and ponder perfection, and ask when is something ever *done*. Slemmons's work is *wabi sabi* – unabashed and meditative. Her paisley necklace or fish brooch, each with components made from old rulers, are never trying to be clever. Ideas, poetry and the love of language (the artist is an enthusiast of Emily Dickinson, for example), are the motor that drives Slemmons to create and find meaningful ways to address issues that are both philosophical and contemporary.

'Paisley' necklace,

by Kiff Slemmons, American, 1998

Wooden rulers and silver

How perfect that the paisley resembles the shape of a bean or comma, two elements that play to Slemmons's strength as a designer: her interest in natural materials and language. The paisley's Indian and Persian origins go back hundreds of years (the 'boteh' teardrop shape dates to ancient times), and it was especially popular in Europe during the eighteenth and nineteenth centuries. For those with shorter memories, the paisley's popularity resurfaced in the 1960s when it showed up on clothing that was part of the psychedelic movement.

'Fish Dream' brooch,

by Kiff Slemmons, American, 1993

Sections of wooden rulers and silver

Sleight-of-hand is never far from any Kiff Slemmons piece of jewelry, but her work is never about exalting wit, but actually draws upon deeper and more conceptual foundations. To best understand Slemmons is to see a body of her work, for as the artists says, 'My materials, often referred to as "found", are above all ideas – ideas proposed and examined through evolving bodies of work ... rather than individual pieces intended as ends in themselves.'

'Venus de Milo' ring, by Christine J. Brandt,
American, c. 2007–8
Hand-carved African black ebony, golden
barite, pyrite crystals and 24K gold leaf

'I give names to my work because I feel it's
important for each piece to have its own
identification. These are like my little children,
and the names help me to keep track of them,
just as you would children. When I was working
on this ring the clam shell shape reminded
me of Botticelli's painting.'

Christine J. Brandt, Embracing the Exotic

She was born in Japan and raised in Europe, Scandinavia and the United States. Perhaps this explains her connection to wood, which she says 'is very comforting', and which, like her, comes from all over the world. Exotic woods such as black ebony from Africa, rosewood cocobolo from South America, lignum vitae from the Caribbean (a wood so hard that it's used for cricket balls) and English pearwood are among the carefully chosen woods used by the artist in her unusual rings, cuffs and necklaces. Each piece of jewelry is hand-carved – no more than fifteen a year are produced – and is rubbed and polished exclusively with Danish oil, thereby respecting the natural integrity of the wood. (Enhancing the wood with chemicals and dyes would be like adding food colouring to a peach.)

A roll call of great artists comes to mind when looking at Christine Brandt's work, especially her sculptural rings. There is the biomorphism of Jean Arp and Brancusi, the distinctive figural forms of Henry Moore. The sprinkling or massing of crystals such as azurite or chrysocolla or vanadinite adds a meditative dressiness, much like the plantings in a Japanese rock garden. Harmony is present in these pieces: each exudes organic forms and a Zen calm.

I think round – I'm attracted to the more organic, billowy shapes. To me, wood is always living. CHRISTINE J. BRANDT

'Cactus Flower' ring, by Christine
J. Brandt, American, 2006
Hand-carved African black ebony and natural
vanadinite crystals

Dainty and demure have no place in the world of
Christine Brandt. In response to nature and her
own interests, the artist makes unique jeweled
expressions in wood. Are the rings large? Very.
Does it matter? No.

The Flexible Art of Liv Blåvarp

'What is it?' wonders the newcomer seeing Liv Blåvarp's jewelry for the first time. With its sinewy construction, weird colour palette and even weirder shapes and clasps, bewilderment about the artist's necklaces and bracelets is justified. Are you looking at an animal or perhaps a plant? (Answer: Both. Or either.) Is this eco-friendly and trendy jewelry or are there some inherently traditional or folk-art elements? No, and yes, but yes with a twist, for this art jewelry embraces Norway's heritage and infuses it with a modern spirit. A small country of only 4,800,000 inhabitants (by comparison, New York City has more than 8 million urban dwellers), Norway has produced playwright Henrik Ibsen, painter Edvard Munch, architect Sverre Fehn and countless Nobel laureates. And its capital, Oslo, is where Liv Blåvarp was raised and educated, save for a year studying art in London.

Gold or silver, stones that are precious or semi-precious are absent in the world of Liv Blåvarp. This is one-note jewelry that produces a wealth of music: exotic woods, some of them hand-dyed and hand-carved, comprise these uniquely imaginative creations. Employing innovative construction, Liv Blåvarp's jewelry is flexible the way that Slinky toys were (in fact the word 'slinky' is Swedish for sleek or sinuous), their moving pieces part of their tactile appeal. Look at a necklace by Liv Blåvarp long enough and soon you'll sense that it moves or breathes, that it's a living thing of natural and immense beauty.

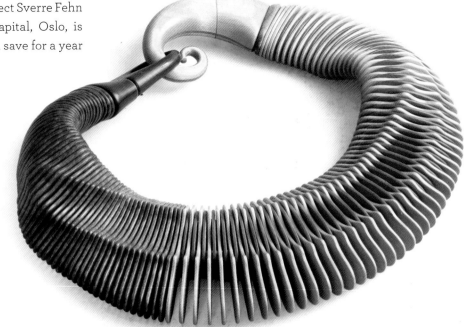

Anthony Roussel, Body Architecture

It would be easy – but a mistake – to call Anthony Roussel a tree hugger. Wood is his medium but not his mantra. For this Englishman, jewelry is art is architecture. The striated bangles and rippled rings he makes are works of sculpture – wearable, sculptural jewelry – with names that evoke built forms (fan and arch) or natural ones (branch and wave). Maybe his work causes others to debate that old chestnut, art versus craft, but not Roussel, who says that he strives to build 'flat elements into fluid structures'. In other words, he's building architecture for the body. He cites as inspiration the rock formations along the English coastline, the layering in the rocks re-imagined in such sustainable woods as birch from Finland or maple from North America. For artist-jewelers such as Roussel, today's world allows for a conscientious use of materials in tandem with advanced technology such as 3-D imaging. Nothing feels forced or phony, and you'd never mistake a Roussel ring for some folksy woodcarving. These are meditations, simulations of movement and being: Roussel's remarkably lithe creations spin and curve or flutter like leaves in the wind, all the while declaring themselves unequivocally creations of the twenty-first century.

'Geo Cork' bangle, by Anthony Roussel,
English, 2008
Layered cork from Portugal
It's Proust and his madeleine redux for the
designer: 'The smell of the cork reminds me
of wine and summers spent in France eating
outside. I want to bring a little of that to
the experience of wearing jewelry.'

Opposite
'Branch' bangle,
by Anthony Roussel, English, 2008
Layered birchwood from Finland
By using wood, Roussel pushes the boundaries
of what is precious in jewelry. Advanced laser
cutting allows him to create thin sheets of wood,
which he then stacks and shapes to produce
these highly articulated forms.

I hope that I've made people consider wood as precious. ANTHONY ROUSSEL

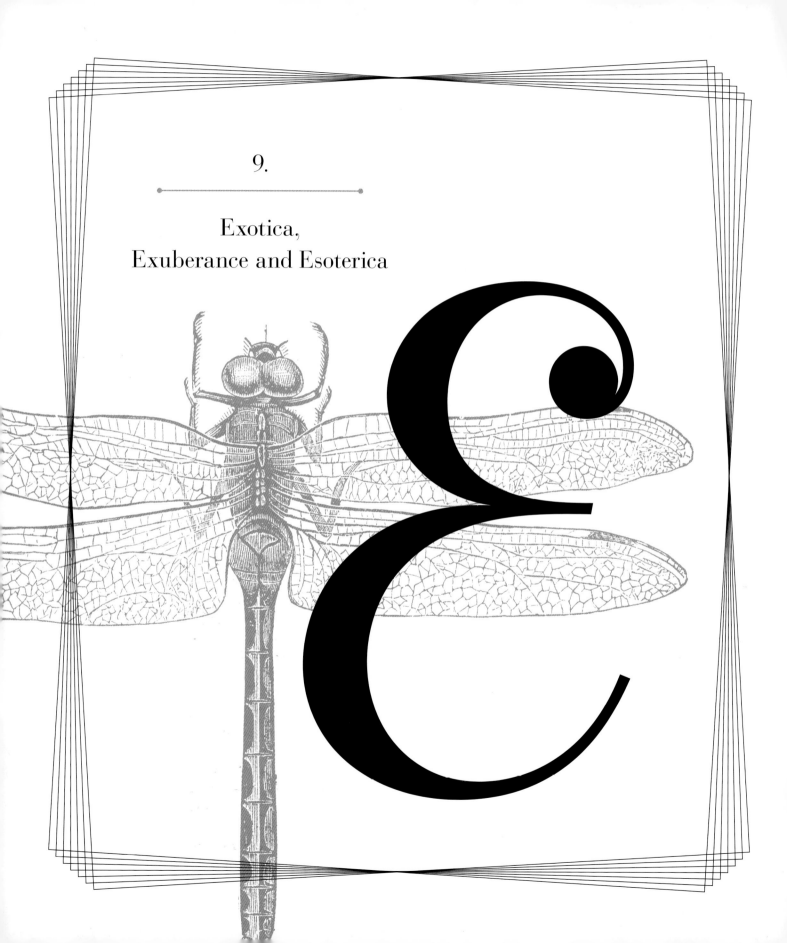

9.

Exotica,
Exuberance and Esoterica

*t*here is a perfume about the word exotica that conjures up mystery and intrigue, like something out of the *Arabian Nights*. It is also a word that, depending how you look at it, yields other interpretations. Drop the 'a' and you have *exotic*, something foreign or unknown, what a scientist classifies as non-native. Swap the 'x' for an 'r' and you get *erotica*, another perfume of sorts, something both sweeter and darker. Overall, exotica is scented with hints of the forbidden and the taboo.

Stag's teeth, tiger claws, hummingbirds, hair from the deceased ... nowadays one shudders at the thought of jewelry made from such things, but for a European of a certain era – roughly the mid-to-late 1800s – these were highly coveted adornments. Nor were they considered morbid, but rather tokens of celebration and commemoration. Claws from tigers, for example, were hunting trophies of game bagged in such faraway places as Africa and Asia; jewelry fashioned from these grand, wild beasts further suggested worldly conquest. As for the nimble, brightly coloured hummingbird, found only in the Americas, myths abound about its supposed supernatural powers. To a lady of a certain means the hummingbird's glistening feathers and tiny stature were adored for adding a chromatic spot of plumage at her neck or dangling from her earlobes.

By the later nineteenth century, the age of Darwin had led to a renewed interest in the natural world, with insects such as the dung beetle a new vogue in jewelry. This industrious beetle, from the family *Scarabaeinae* (insect order *Coleoptera*), forms balls of manure (hence the name), which it also feasts on. But this was no ordinary bug and its history added to its renewed lustre. The ancient Egyptians designated a specific scarab, the *Scarabaeus sacer*, as sacred; to them it was allied with the sun god who signified transformation or rebirth, a reason it was often buried with the dead to ensure an afterlife. They also considered the scarab an amulet, worn by both rich and poor. By the 1800s, this sacred scarab was being fashioned into novel and eye-catching jewelry – one of the more

superb examples is the rare South American scarab necklace, page 217, which features twenty-five scarabs in graduated sizes, a potent good luck charm for those who believed in the power of myth.

As Darwin rocked the civilized world with his theories of natural selection, wanderlust and education with a capital *E* had struck Europeans – especially the British – followed shortly thereafter by Americans. Extended travel that began in the 1700s was flourishing by the 1800s: upper-class men and women made the Grand Tour by steamer and later by railway and automobile. Such travels were an opportunity to 'get' culture by seeing it firsthand, and also to make purchases intended to buttress one's pedigree and status. The general itinerary included France, Switzerland and Italy, the latter particularly rich with antiquities. Though Rome was regarded as the cultural zenith of one's journey, local stops often included Naples and the smaller neighbouring towns of Pompeii and Herculaneum, newly excavated in the mid-1700s, revealing a hitherto buried time capsule. It was only a matter of time before lava jewelry – a local souvenir – was purchased, further attesting to the reawakened interest in classical architecture and sculpture. The neoclassical movement had begun in earnest, and with it were created scads of intricately carved jewelry from coral, shell and lava depicting an alphabet of Greek and Roman mythology.

Back home, a different sort of wave had gathered strength, and that was sentimental jewelry, including hair jewelry, often described as mourning or memorial jewelry. Like the painter of miniatures so fashionable in the late 1700s and early 1800s, the hairworker operated on a scale of delicate and exacting proportions. Some designs were tucked into small lockets or into memorial rings inscribed with sayings or the name of the deceased. In America, the most famous treasured locks are those from George Washington, the first president of the United States. Today they are stored at his ancestral home of Mount Vernon in Virginia. But style, like life, ebbs and flows, and not all hair jewelry was for gloomy occasions – in time it was also fashioned for engagements and weddings.

Taste and values have changed greatly since much of this exotic jewelry was made. Our current stance is to post a figurative 'Do Not Disturb' sign over our feathered and furred friends, and to preserve our antiquities from loot or loss. A woman's hair, however, is still prey to countless dreams and desires.

Previous page
Iridescent scarab brooch, c. 1880
Scarab beetle shell and gold
In Franz Kafka's Metamorphosis *(1915),
the servant of the Samson household refers
to the transformed protagonist, Gregor, as a
dung beetle, though translators and scholars
have often differed on whether he was
specifically a dung beetle (sacred scarab)
or just a city cockroach.*

Above left
**Butterfly brooch, Austro-Hungarian,
c. late 19th to early 20th century
South American Blue Morpho butterfly
wings (*Morpho Menelaus*), diamonds,
rubies, glass and gold**
*The phrase 'Butterflies are free' originates
in Charles Dickens's* Bleak House *(1852–53),
that dark story of Victorian England, though
butterflies have been widely celebrated in
literature and poetry by many. In the art world,
perhaps the best-known association with
lepidopterans is James McNeill Whistler,
whose signature was a stylized butterfly.*

Above right
**Butterfly brooch, c. late 19th century
Butterfly wings, diamonds, glass and gold**
Butterflies are the leitmotif of the novella
Morpho Eugenia *by A. S. Byatt (adapted in 1995
as the movie* Angels and Insects*), a moody love
story set in the mid-1800s, around the time that
insect jewelry became fashionable.*

'Lunaria' necklace (and detail),
by Jennifer Trask, American, c. 2005
Money plant (*Lunaria annua*), moonstones,
diamonds, python skin, dragonfly wings, mica,
ficus leaf skeleton, 18K and 22K gold
and palladium

Jennifer Trask:
A Modern Miniaturist

Artist Jennifer Trask takes the nineteenth-century preoccupation with nature (including insects) and investigates it from the viewpoint of a twenty-first-century artist. Her 'scientific samples' are encased in disks covered with old watch crystals.

'Green Magenta Beetles' brooch,
by Jennifer Trask, American, 2006
Brazilian leaf beetle (*Chrysomelidae*),
rhodalite, tourmaline, 18K and 22K gold

'Japanese Quatrefoil' brooch
by Jennifer Trask, American, 2001
Japanese rose beetles, 22K and 18K gold,
silver back plate

This page
'Sea Change' brooch (two views),
by Jennifer Trask, American, c. 2006
Silver, steel and peacock feathers

Opposite left
'Spring' necklace,
by Jennifer Trask, American, 2005
Ornithoptera priamus urvillianus, Giant
Blue Swallowtail (*Papillio zalmoxis*), Green
Birdwing (*Ornithoptera priamus poseidon*),
Malaysian butterfly, blue topaz, cerulean blue,
fluorite, peridot, permanent green, crushed
green quartz, mica, Riman's green pigment,
powdered malachite, aquamarine, 22K gold,
sterling and fine silver

It exhibits in its form the beautiful plumage of the peacock, the shadings of the hummingbird, the bill of the crane, and the short legs of the swallow. OLIVER GOLDSMITH, 1855

The Kingfisher, 'King of Fishers'

Its nickname is the flying jewel. Hailed for its iridescent deep blue and turquoise feathers, the kingfisher has a notably long beak and rather stout legs, and ranges in size from 4 to 17 inches (10 to 43 cm). This distinctive bird is happiest when alone though it doesn't shirk the responsibilities of parenthood, which can be rigorous, and is earnestly monogamous. When it comes to mealtime, its m.o. is a sit-and-wait approach, though once engaged its characteristic vertical dive into water delivers a satisfying near 100 per cent return on investment, typically small fish (earning it yet another nickname, the 'king of fishers'). But the kingfisher isn't terribly picky, and enjoys a 'surf and turf' diet, including reptiles, insects and small mammals such as mice. There are more than one hundred species of kingfishers worldwide, eleven of them occurring in China. All of them belong to the order *Coraciiformes*. The word halcyon derives from the Greek for kingfisher, which Pliny and Aristotle each reference in their writings – the bird was believed to nest on the water and to possess the innate ability to calm both wind and wave. However apocryphal, there is indeed a genus of kingfisher known as Halcyon.

Of the kingfisher, the naturalist Oliver Goldsmith opined, 'Even those that are tyrants by nature never spread capricious destruction; and, unlike man, never inflict a pain but when urged by necessity.'

Kingfisher tiara,
Chinese, c. 1880–1900
Kingfisher feathers and gilded copper alloy
This ornament and the one below were likely once worn by the empress dowager, the effective ruler of China during the later years of the Qing Dynasty.

Kingfisher phoenix hair ornament,
Chinese, c. 19th century
Kingfisher feathers, pearls, glass beads, rubies, gilded silver and silver thread
'The entire bird is used, and is mounted on wires and springs that permit the head and wings to be moved about in the most natural manner.' Harper's Bazaar, *1875. In this piece, the small phoenixes represent the empress.*

Opposite
Kingfisher wedding tiara, c. 1830
Kingfisher feathers and gold
Matrimonial grandeur was bestowed on the young bride who wore this exceptional plumage in her hair.

Kingfisher Jewelry, a Mania for Magnificence

As far back as the Han Dynasty (206 BC–220 AD), the Chinese have been uniquely identified with the azure blue and turquoise feathers of the kingfisher in decoration and ornament. Fans, ceremonial robes, bedcovers, earrings, wedding headdresses, even three-inch-long fingernail guards were decorated with exquisitely blue kingfisher feathers. Although their use by the Chinese dates back millennia, the apogee of kingfisher mania and magnificence came in the Qing dynasty (1644–1912), during the Manchu reign, when the feathers were used for the most stunning hair ornaments. Depending on the wearer's rank, the kingfisher feathers would be mounted on gold or silver and embellished with pearls and such precious or semi-precious stones as rubies, sapphires, coral, Peking glass and jade. The effect was anything but ordinary and the magnificence of a piece often served to indicate social status and political muscle. Power, it seems, could be communicated by the finest fluttering of plumage, a grace note seen and understood by all.

From early boyhood, I have been almost a monomaniac on hummingbirds.

MARTIN JOHNSON HEADE

Hummingbirds, 'Gems of Nature'

By the 1860s and 1870s a taste for the exotic appealed to women of style, including the wearing of gem-set hummingbird jewelry. Most of the birds mounted probably came from Mexico and South America, where the hummingbird was especially brightly coloured. In his book *Travels of a Naturalist* (1894), the French naturalist Adolphe Boucard describes his first glimpse of this diminutive creature in Valparaiso as 'one of the most remarkable epochs of my life'. He writes that hummingbirds 'surpass in brilliancy and in variety of colours, that of the most precious stones, such as rubies, emeralds, topazes, amethysts, turquoises, sapphires, garnets, etc. They are the unequalled gems of Nature.' For Boucard, their beauty was best admired in situ

rather than after a visit to the taxidermist, and he argues persuasively for their undisturbed life in the wild.

It's easy to be enchanted by these nectar-driven birds. As Boucard reported, their nests are the size of walnuts and their eggs are like peas, further attesting to the fact that they are the world's smallest bird. However, with 343 species the hummingbird is amazingly the second largest family of birds. During normal flight, hummingbirds can beat their wings as much as eighty times per second and when courting, their swooning dives race up to 60 miles an hour. Most surprising fact of all, given their predilection for sipping the nectar of flowers: they have no sense of smell.

Harry Emanuel, a Flair for the Fantastic

He was listed as 'HE, Court Jeweler, to the Queen and to the Prince and Princess of Wales, Author of *Diamonds and Precious Stones: Their History, Value and Distinguishing Characteristics*, 1865.' HE was Harry Emanuel, renowned London jeweler and one of the city's largest dealers in diamonds. Emanuel took over his father's business in 1855 when he was scarcely twenty-five and a decade later followed his work in ivory with jewelry made from feathers. He patented a technique that involved gluing feathers to prepared mounts using shellac. A visitor to his shop recalled seeing the heads of hummingbirds mounted in necklaces and earrings alongside richly decorated cabinets filled with silver and gold, and other spectacular objects. Emanuel himself was nearly as exotic as the objects he made: in 1867 he exhibited a life-size automated musical silver swan at the 1867 Paris International Exhibition, which caught the fancy of Mark Twain, who later wrote about it in his book, *The Innocents Abroad*. Upon retirement, Emanuel purchased a Portuguese title and moved with his wife to Paris; by 1880 he had appointed himself the Minister Plenipotentiary (ambassador) of the Dominican Republic in France. Harry Emanuel died in Nice in 1898.

Hummingbird ear pendants, by Harry Emanuel, English, c. 1865
Hummingbird heads, red glass eyes and gold
Among some Native American and South American cultures this tiny creature is believed to bring joy, healing, success in war, and rain.

Claw brooch, c. 1880

Tiger claws and gold

Hunting big game animals in India was a sport greatly enjoyed by the colonial rulers of the British Raj. Trophy jewelry included tiger claws, in this case distinguished by gold and the elaborate detailing heralding the magnificent beast. Pieces such as this may have been made in Calcutta and bought as souvenirs.

Tiger's claw lady's wristwatch, by Cartier, French, c. 1925

Tiger claw, enamel, coral, sapphire and gold

Surely one of the more unusual pieces of jewelry from the great house of Cartier, although animals have always to one degree or another been associated with the jeweler. This lithe watch, which pandered to the taste for big game hunting and safaris, was released about a decade prior to the publication of Out of Africa, *the memoir by Isak Dinesen (the nom de plume of the Dane Karen von Blixen) of her years living in Kenya.*

Stag's teeth bracelet, German, c. 1930

Stag's teeth and aluminium

*More than a conversation piece, this bangle
is an unusual and exceptional example
of trophy jewelry.*

Tooth pendant, early 20th century

Animal teeth and gold

*As with claws, teeth were also turned into
jewelry, and in this case there is one central
tooth with four teeth, on either side.*

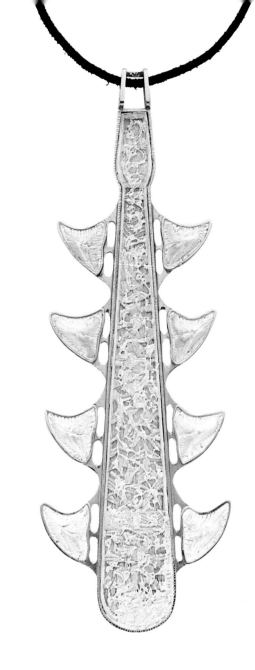

*Never attack a tiger on foot – if you can help it.
There are cases in which you must do so. Then
face him like a Briton, and kill him if you can;
for if you fail to kill him he will certainly kill you.*

WALTER CAMPBELL, MY INDIAN JOURNAL, 1864

Grand Tour Spoils

It was in AD 79 that Vesuvius blew its top and lava rained down on the villages of Pompeii and Herculaneum, forever sealing off life there. For Europeans and Americans, the relics from Vesuvius were part of the allure as they made their way through the south of Italy in the 1700 and 1800s while making the Grand Tour.

In some ways, 'grand' was a misnomer, for accommodation and travel were often rather simple, bordering on primitive. As one gentleman in the late eighteenth century observed while in Sicily, 'There is not a wheel in the whole country.' Moreover, tourists kept bumping into, well, other tourists – 'the town is perfectly filled with English', complained one unhappy English traveller in Rome around the same time. But for all such discontents, the classical antiquities of Rome and nearby Pompeii, especially, were sources of revelation.

Hardier tourists described climbing Vesuvius, its volcanic crater still steaming, with occasional rivulets of fire streaming down the mountain. For those with more material interests, it was the accumulation of ancient sculpture and other objets d'art that made their hearts race. The Grand Tour was like a great shopping spree, especially for Americans who, despite their new wealth and colossal estates, felt that the purchase of jewelry and classical statues would give them history – an enviable given among their European counterparts.

Lava bracelet, Italian, mid-19th century

Lava cameos and gold

Varying shades of lava's natural palette
– dusty whites and beiges to oyster grey and a
ruddy brown – are used to visual effect in this
raised cameo carving depicting the gods of the
planets, arranged in order of their relationship
to the seven days of the week. From the left are
Diana, the moon, for Monday; Mars for Tuesday;
Mercury for Wednesday; Jupiter for Thursday;
Venus for Friday; Saturn for Saturday;
and Apollo for Sunday.

Diana the Huntress lava brooch,

c. 1860

Lava cameo and gold

The artist who made this piece from the
lava that engulfed a great civilization gave
back in kind by depicting one of the greatest
of Roman goddesses, Diana the huntress.
With her quiver and bow, and dog by her side,
Diana is recognized as the virgin
goddess of animals and woodland,
and the patron of the hunt.

Maltese Cross piqué ear pendants,

c. 1860

Bog oak and gold

For a time, bog oak was considered another
suitable material for mourning jewelry, and
was often less expensive than jet, which was
also much darker. Whereas jet was chiefly
an English product, bog oak came from
peat bogs in Ireland.

Bog oak brooch, c. 1860

Bog oak and gold

These dogs are most likely greyhounds, classified
in 1570 by Shakespeare's contemporary, John
Caius, as hunting dogs. In England they have
been used to chase down deer, foxes and stags,
though their favourite quarry seems to be the
English hare.

'Osorio Lobo' pendant,

by Kiff Slemmons, American, 2006

Mouse bones, beeswax and sterling silver

The inspiration is the Lupanar, the largest
surviving brothel at Pompeii, also known as
the 'den of wolves'. There the pleasure-seeking
Pompeiian male had his choice of ten stone
'beds', his antics depicted on the walls, making
them among the earliest of erotic frescoes.
Kiff Slemmons, who had visited Pompeii,
made this pendant with mouse bones that she
painstakingly removed from owl pellets in order
to study their diet in Washington State.
The mouse bones were then embedded
in beeswax and framed in silver.

Of all keepsakes, memorials, relics – most dearly, most devotedly, do I love a little lock of hair. ANONYMOUS, c. 1850

Hairwork flower brooch, c. 1820–30

Woven hair and gold

The best hairworkers, as these women were known, excelled at turning locks into dazzling displays of design such as this superb helix of spun hair made to resemble the petals of a flower. But the pièce de résistance of hairworking was a life-size depiction of Queen Victoria, made entirely from human hair, displayed at the Paris Exposition of 1855.

Hairwork bracelet, c. 1790–1810

Woven hair, enamel, seed pearls and gold

As hair jewelry became an industry, some firms were known to substitute the hair of the deceased with similarly 'available' hair in the shop. To prevent such chicanery, young girls at home were taught the craft to ensure that only the hair of the intended was actually used. A popular manual was The Jeweller's Book of Patterns in Hairwork *by William Halford and Charles Young, published in London, 1864.*

**Memorial ring commemorating two siblings,
English, c. 1804–5**

Woven hair, enamel, seed pearls and gold

*This memorial ring commemorates the death
of two siblings, their names inscribed in gold on
the ring, and lockets of their hair divided among
the two compartments under the bezel. Around
the time this ring was made, it was customary
to give such tokens at a funeral gathering.
The sisters were nineteen and twenty, and
still unmarried, as attested by the use of white
– symbolizing purity – for the enamel.*

**Elephant hair bracelet, Van Cleef & Arpels,
French, c. 1970s**

Elephant hair and 18K gold

*Elephant ivory isn't the only part of these
beloved beasts used for jewelry – even a firm as
established as Van Cleef & Arpels used elephant
hair, as in this great-looking link bracelet.
It was all part of the 'back to the land'
movement prevalent in the 1970s.*

Cuff, by Cartier London, c. 1970s

Elephant hair, white gold and diamonds

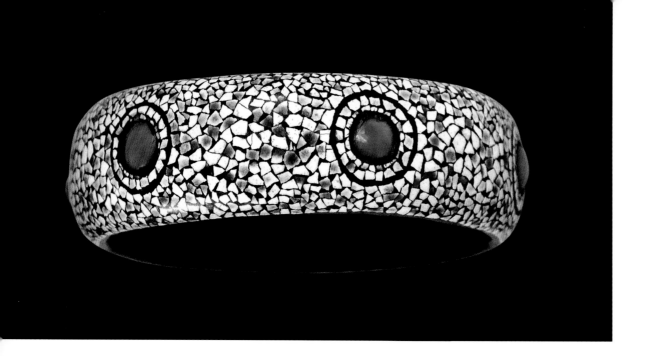

**'Coquille d'Oeuf' bangle,
by Marcel Wolfers, Belgian, c. 1925
Crushed eggshells, wood and cabochon corals**

*At the time this eggshell crackle bangle was
made, a similar finish was appearing on Art
Deco French furniture made by the great
Emile-Jacques Ruhlmann, who sniffed 'Only
the very rich can pay for what is new and they
alone can make it fashionable.' For a specially
commissioned black lacquer dressing table,
Ruhlmann collaborated with Jean Dunand
who designed a Cubist pattern using
crushed white eggshells, which he embedded
into the inky lacquer.*

Stingray cuff, by Kara Ross,
American, 2009
Stingray, gold and diamonds

Shagreen ear clips and brooch set,
by Fabrice, French, c. early 1980s
Shagreen and silver
Shagreen is one of those materials considered
a luxury, and is most often used for boxes.
It is actually the dried skin, or leather,
of the ray family.

Opposite
Fossil brooch, by Margret Craver,
American, 1985
Cross-section of fossilized nautilus,
gold foil and silver
Although Margret Craver is identified with the
American Studio Jewelry Movement and its
beginnings in the 1950s, this association came
about more by happenstance than by intent.
Craver began taking art classes in the 1920s,
but she was largely on her own when it came to
learning metalsmithing. She was a modernist
unafraid to take from the past, as when she
reintroduced a technique little known in its day,
en resille, a method of applying enamel with
metal backing onto glass. By 1980 she had turned
to a new interest that began to show in her work:
the natural world. It was during this time that
Craver made this unusual brooch.

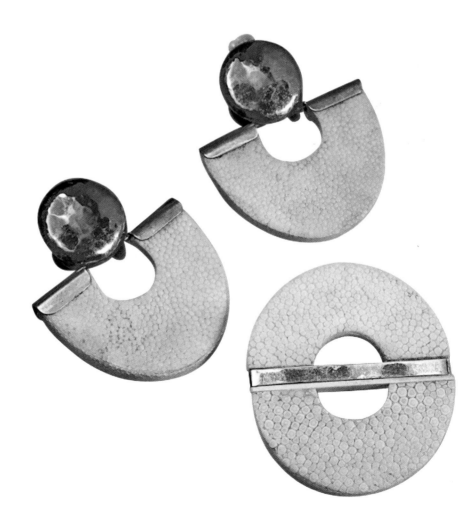

Scarab brooch and ear pendants, c. 1870

Scarab beetle shells and 15K gold

By the time that Darwin's ideas were being debated along with new botanical discoveries, an interest in jewelry resembling insects or flowers was newly fashionable. In this case, actual beetles were incorporated after having been dried and treated with a protective coating. For the stylish woman of the 1800s, this brooch and pair of earrings were very much au courant.

Opposite

Scarab fringe necklace, c. 1860

South American scarab beetle shells and 18K gold

To the ancient Egyptians, the scarab represented the renewal of life; to the nineteenth-century Europeans, it came to represent happiness and longevity. This fringe necklace is an excellent example of the use of multiples: while beads may be sorted and strung according to size, here the selection process must have required extraordinary patience and good luck to come up with so many perfect beetles in such flawless alignment.

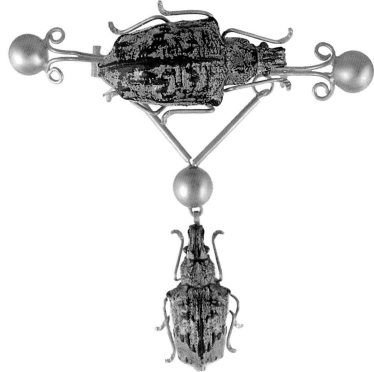

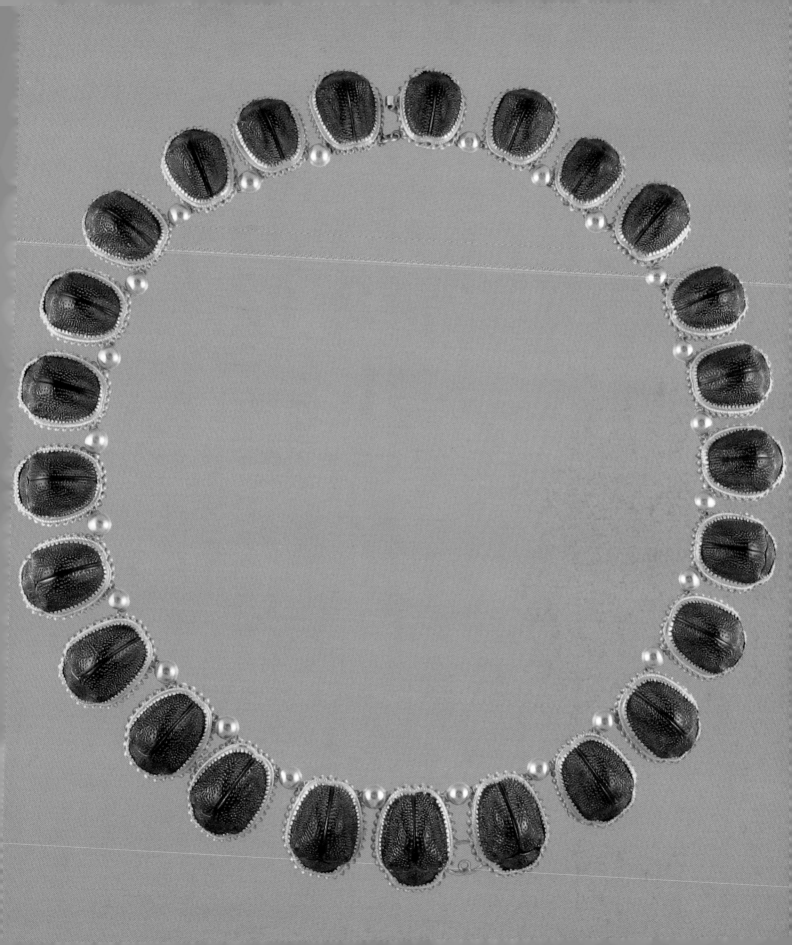

Selected Bibliography

Barber, Richard, and Anne Riches. *A Dictionary of Fabulous Beasts*. New York: Walker & Company, 1971.

Batchen, Geoffrey. *Forget Me Not: Photography & Remembrance*. New York: Princeton Architectural Press, 2004.

Becker, Vivian. *Art Nouveau Jewelry*. London: Thames & Hudson, 1998.

—. *The Jewelry of René Lalique*. London: the Goldsmith's Company, 1987.

Bender, Marilyn. 'Now, Even the Rich Can Have Costume Jewelry'. *New York Times*, 17 October 1966: 45.

Benfey, Christopher. *A Summer of Hummingbirds: Love, Art, and Scandal in the Intersecting Worlds of Emily Dickinson, Mark Twain, Harriet Beecher Stowe, and Martin Johnson Heade*. New York: Penguin Press, 2008.

Bennett, David, and Daniela Mascetti. *Understanding Jewelry*. Rev. ed. London: Antique Collectors' Club, 2000.

Bizot, Chantal et al. *The Jewels of Jean Schlumberger*. New York: Abrams, 2001.

Black, Jeremy. *Italy and the Grand Tour*. New Haven, CT: Yale University Press, 2003.

Blumberg, Jess. 'A Brief History of the Amber Room'. *Smithsonian.com*, 1 August 2007.

Brubach, Holly. *A Dedicated Follower of Fashion*. London: Phaidon, 1999.

Buffum, Arnold W. *The Tears of the Heliades: Or Amber as a Gem*. Rev. ed. New York: G. P. Putnam's Sons; London: Sampson Low, Marston & Co., Ltd., 1900.

Cailles, Françoise. *Merveilleuses Perles*. Luxembourg: Argus Valentines, 2006.

—. *René Boivin, Jeweller*. London: Quartet Books, 1994.

Cederwall, Sandraline, and Hal Riney. *Spratling Silver*. San Francisco: Chronicle Books, 1990.

Cirlot, J. E. *A Dictionary of Symbols*. 2nd ed., trans. by Jack Sage. New York: Philosophical Library, 1981.

Corbett, Patricia. *Verdura: The Life and Work of a Master Jeweler*. London: Thames & Hudson, 2002.

Dawes, Ginny Redington, and Corinne Davidov. *Victorian Jewelry: Unexplored Treasures*. Photographs by Tom Dawes. New York: Abbeville Press Publishers, 1991.

—, with Olivia Collings. *Georgian Jewellery: 1714–1830*. Suffolk, UK: Antique Collectors' Club, 2007.

Dietz, Ulysses Grant, ed. *The Glitter and the Gold: Fashioning America's Jewelry*. Exh. cat. Newark, NJ: Newark Museum of Art, 1997.

Duncan, Alastair. *Art Deco Complete: The Definitive Guide to the Decorative Arts of the 1920s and 1930s*. London: Thames & Hudson, 2009.

Esten, John. *Diana Vreeland: The Bazaar Years*. New York: Universe, 2001.

Fales, Martha Gandy. *Jewelry in America, 1600–1900*. Suffolk, UK: Antique Collectors' Club, 1995.

Ferreira, Dr Maria Teresa Gomes, ed., in collaboration with Dr Maria Fernanda Passos Leite, Dr Maria Isabel Pereira Coutinho, and Mary P. Proddow. *Art Nouveau Jewelry by René Lalique*. Exh. cat. Washington, D.C.: International Exhibition Foundation, 1985.

Finlay, Victoria. *Jewels: A Secret History*. New York: Ballantine Books, 2006.

Fiorelli, Anna. *Corals and Cameos: The Treasures of Torre del Greco*. Exh. cat. New York: Fashion Institute of Technology, 1989.

Flower, Margaret. *Victorian Jewellery*. South Brunswick, NJ: A. S. Barnes, 1967.

Foshay, Ella M. *Reflections of Nature: Flowers in American Art*. Exh. cat., Whitney Museum of American Art, New York. New York: Knopf, 1984.

Gage, Elizabeth. *The Unconventional Gage*. Privately published, 2003.

Garside, Anne, ed. *Jewelry: Ancient to Modern*. New York: Viking Press in association with the Walters Art Museum, 1979.

Gere, Charlotte. *Victorian Jewelry Design*. Chicago: Henry Regnery Co., 1972.

Greenhalgh, Peter, ed. *The Persistence of Craft*. London: A & C Black Publishers, Ltd., 2002.

Grimaldi, David. *Amber*. New York: Abrams, 2002.

Hardwick, Paula. *Discovering Horn*. Guildford, UK: Lutterworth Press, 1989.

Harrison, Stephen, Emmanuel Ducamp and Jeannine Falino. *Artistic Luxury: Fabergé, Tiffany, and Lalique*. Exh. cat., Cleveland Museum of Art and Fine Arts Museums of San Francisco. Cleveland/New Haven: Cleveland Museum of Art in association with Yale University Press, 2008.

Head, Edith, and Paddy Calistro. *Edith Head's Hollywood*, foreword by Bette Davis. New York: E.P. Dutton, Inc., 1983.

Hemenway, Priya. *Divine Proportion: In Art, Nature and Science*. New York: Sterling, 2005.

Hinks, Peter. *Twentieth-Century British Jewellery: 1900–1980*. London: Faber and Faber, 1983.

Hughes, Graham. 'Andrew Grima'. *The Independent*, 18 January 2008.

JAR. Exh. cat., Somerset House, London. London: Art Books International, 2002.

Jutheau, Viviane. *Sterlé*. Paris: Editions Vecteurs, 1991.

Landman, Neil H., Paula M. Mikkelsen, Rüdiger Bieler, and Bennet Bronson. *Pearls: A Natural History*. Exh. cat., American Museum of Natural History, New York, and The Field Museum, Chicago. New York: Abrams, in association with the American Museum of Natural History and The Field Museum, 2001.

Lemonick, Michael D. 'Forever Amber'. *Time* magazine, vol. 147, no. 7, 12 February 1996.

Loring, John. *Paulding Farnham: Tiffany's Lost Genius*. New York: Abrams, 2000.

Luthi, Ann Louise. *Sentimental Jewelry: Antique Jewels of Love and Sorrow*. Buckinghamshire, UK: Shire Publications, 2007.

Markowitz, Yvonne M., and Elyse Zorn Karlin. *Imperishable Beauty: Art Nouveau Jewelry*. Exh. cat. Boston: Museum of Fine Arts, 2008.

—, and Susan Ward. 'Art Nouveau Jewelry'. *The Magazine Antiques*, July 2008.

McLanathan, Richard. *The Art of Marguerite Stix*. New York: Abrams, 1977.

Menkes, Suzy. 'All that Sparkles from a Princess's Life'. *International Herald Tribune*, 31 May 2006.

—. *The Windsor Style*. Topsfield, MA: Salem House Publishers, 1987.

Milbank, Caroline Rennolds. *Couture Accessory*. New York: Abrams, 2002.

—. *Couture: The Great Designers*. New York: Stewart, Tabori & Chang, 1985.

Munn, Geoffrey. *Tiaras: A History of Splendour*. London: Antique Collectors' Club, 2001.

Nadelhoffer, Eric. *Cartier*. Repr. London: Thames & Hudson; San Francisco: Chronicle Books, 2007.

Nemy, Enid. 'David Webb Heralds New Age'. *New York Times*, 28 June 1967: 40.

O'Day, Deirdre. *Victorian Jewellery*. London: Charles Letts Books, Ltd., 1974.

Papi, Stefano, and Alexandra Rhodes. *Famous Jewelry Collectors*. London: Thames & Hudson; New York: Abrams, 1999.

Pedersen, Maggie Campbell. *Gem and Ornamental Materials of Organic Origin*. Oxford, UK: Elsevier, 2004.

Phillips, Clare, ed. *Bejewelled by Tiffany 1837–1987*. With contributions by Vivienne Becker, Ulysses Grant Dietz, Alice Cooney Frelinghuysen, John Loring and Katherine Purcell. Exh. cat., Gilbert Collection, London. New Haven, CT: Yale University Press in association with the Gilbert Collection Trust and Tiffany & Co., 2006.

Phillips, Phoebe, ed. *Ivory: An International History and Illustrated Survey*. New York: Abrams, 1987.

Possémé, Evelyne, and Laurence Mouillefarine. *Art Deco Jewelry: Modern Masterworks and Their Makers*. London: Thames & Hudson, 2009.

Proddow, Penny, and Deborah Healy. *American Jewelry: Glamour and Tradition*. New York: Rizzoli, 1987.

Raulet, Sylvie. *Art Deco Jewelry*. London: Thames & Hudson; New York: Rizzoli, 1985.

—. *Van Cleef & Arpels*. New York: Rizzoli, 1987.

Robinson, Ruth. 'Sea Shells and Gems to Adorn a Finger or a Table Top'. *New York Times*, 17 November 1972: 54.

Rower, Alexander S. C., and Holton Rower, eds. *Calder Jewelry*. New Haven, CT: Yale University Press, 2007.

Rudoe, Judy. *Cartier, 1900–1939*. Exh. cat., Metropolitan Museum of Art, New York, and the British Museum, London. New York: Abrams, 1999.

Sataloff, Joseph. *Art Nouveau Jewelry*. Bryn Mawr, PA: Dorrance, 1984.

Scarisbrick, Diana. *Ancestral Jewels*. New York: Vendome, 1989.

Schon, Marbeth. *Modernist Jewelry, 1930–60: The Wearable Art Movement*. Altgen, PA: Schiffer, 2004.

Snowman, Kenneth. *The Master Jewelers*. London: Thames & Hudson; New York: Abrams, 1990.

Stix, Hugh, and Marguerite Stix, with R. Tucker Abbott. *The Shell: 500 Million Years of Inspired Design*. Photographs by H. Landshoff. New York: Abrams, 1978.

Taylor, Elizabeth. *Elizabeth Taylor: My Love Affair with Jewelry*. Edited by Ruth A. Peltason. London: Thames &

Hudson; New York: Simon & Schuster, 2002.

Thomas, Ingrid. *The Shell: A World of Decoration and Ornament*. London and New York: Thames & Hudson, 2007.

Triossi, Amanda, ed. *Bulgari: Between Eternity and History, from 1884 to 2009, 125 Years of Italian Jewels*. Milan: Skira Editore, 2009.

Vaill, Amanda, and Janet Zapata. *Seaman Schepps: A Century of New York Jewelry Design*. New York: Vendome, 2004.

Van Cleef & Arpels. *The Spirit of Beauty*. Exh. cat., Mori Arts Center Gallery, Tokyo. France: Éditions Xavier Barral, 2009.

Vever, Henri. *French Jewelry of the Nineteenth Century*. Trans. Katherine Purcell. London and New York: Thames & Hudson, 2001.

Vreeland, Diana. *DV*. New York: Knopf, 1984.

White, T. H., ed. *The Book of Beasts, Being a Translation from a London Bestiary of the Twelfth Century*. London: Jonathan Cape, 1954.

Wilson, Francis, and Caroline Crisford, eds. *The Belle Epoque of French Jewellery: 1850–1910*. London: T. Heneage, 1991.

Yelavich, Susan, and Don Freeman. *Ted Muehling: A Portrait by Don Freeman*. New York: Rizzoli, 2008.

Picture Credits

———————●———————

The author and publisher wish to thank those individuals, firms and museums that so kindly allowed the reproduction of images noted below. In particular, we wish to acknowledge the enormous help from Corbis for images on behalf of Christie's. We have made every effort to credit any and all sources. Specific photograph credits are also noted in the information below, with special thanks to Samuel Bristow, John Bigelow Taylor, David Behl and Loring McAlpin.

Courtesy À La Vieille Russie, New York: 34 above, 97 below; Courtesy Anaconda, Paris: 57 right; Courtesy Lorenz Bäumer, Paris: 134, 135; Courtesy Alexis Bittar: 186; Courtesy Liv Blåvarp/Charon Kransen Arts, New York (photo Audbjørn Rønning): 195 below; Courtesy Bonhams, New York and London: 125, 130 below, 148 all; Bonhams & Butterfields: 17 below; Courtesy Christine J. Brandt: 194 above (photo © Samuel Bristow), 194 below (photo Michael Brandt); The Trustees of the British Museum: 76 left; Bulgari Vintage Collection, Courtesy Bulgari Historical Archive, Rome: 38, 39 above left and below, 120; Courtesy Bulgari Historical Archive, Rome: 145 top left; Courtesy Jill Burkee: 92; Collection Camilla Dietz Bergeron (photos © Samuel Bristow): 33 top right, 100 bottom left, 128 bottom right; Collection Camilla Dietz Bergeron, Ltd. and Symbolic & Chase (photo courtesy Christie's Images/Corbis): 36; Courtesy Camilla Dietz Bergeron, Ltd.: 56 bottom right, 83 left; (photos © Samuel Bristow) 50, 57 below, 58 above, 76 right, private collection 121, 145 below right, 153 above and right, 155, 157; Courtesy Christie's Images/Corbis: 19 both, 20 above, 28, 30 above left and above right, 32 above, 39 right, 40 right, 42, 43 both, 45 below, 56 above, 65 left, 73, 79, 81 above, 82 centre, 83 right, 86 above and below, 97 above left and above right, 98 both, 99 below, 100 above and below right, 101 above left and above right, 104 above left and above right, 106, 107 all, 108 left and above right, 110 below, 112 all, 113 all, 114 above, 118, 122 above and left, 123 above and below right, 132, 133, 150, 162, 163 below left, 170, 174 below, 184 above left, 200 both, 208 below left, 209, 221; Courtesy Christie's Images/Corbis © 2010 Artists Rights Society (ARS), New York/ADAGP, Paris: 63, 66 below, 68 right, 78, 178 both; Courtesy Marilyn Cooperman (photos Art Boonparn): 126 all; Courtesy Paolo Costagli: 59, 89; Courtesy Jessica Kagan Cushman: 93 below; Collection Francesca Romana Davis (photos © Samuel Bristow): 153 below, 154; Collection Gabriella De Ferrari (photos © Samuel Bristow): 35, 75 left; Courtesy de Grisogono: 54; Courtesy Dior Couture, Paris: 61; Courtesy Fourtané (photo Kristofar

Bonifas): 30 below; Courtesy Fred Leighton, New York (photos © Samuel Bristow): 55, 84, 103 above, 105, 142 below, 167; Courtesy Elizabeth Gage: 23; Courtesy Lee Hale (photos Loring McAlpin): 191 both; Courtesy Hancock's, London: 45 above, 115 above; Hancock's, courtesy Van Cleef & Arpels: 32 below; Courtesy Marion Harris, New York (photos © John Peden):160 left, 171 below, 215 below; Courtesy Hemmerle, Munich: 1 and 129 both, 184 below; Courtesy Hermès (photo Studio des Fleurs): 70; Courtesy Mesi Jilly: 138; Courtesy Robin Katz Vintage Jewels, New York: above right, 57 above, 74, 213 above; Courtesy Gabriella Kiss: 7, 71 (photo Loring McAlpin); Courtesy Kentshire Galleries, New York: 25, 26, 51 above left, 110 right, 142 above, 164 above and below left, 165 both, 171 above, 199, 208 above left and centre, 210 below, 211 above and below left, 216, 217; Courtesy Kentshire Galleries, New York/private collection: 204, 212 above; Courtesy Rebecca Koven, New York: 20 below; Courtesy Larkspur & Hawk, New York: 139 left; Collection Daphne Lingon (photo © Samuel Bristow): 164 right; Courtesy Macklowe Gallery, New York (photo © Daniel Root): 17 above, 34 right, 99 above, 122 right, 174 above; Courtesy Mobilia Gallery, Cambridge, Mass.: 179 below (photo Cindy Brennan), 201; Courtesy Ted Muehling (photos Loring McAlpin): 22, 93 above, 95; Museum of Fine Arts, Boston (Photographs © 2010 Museum of Fine Arts, Boston): (Bequest of William Arnold Buffum) 13, 14–15; (The Daphne Farago Collection) 179 above, 190, 192, 193, 195 above, 214 below; (The Elizabeth Day McCormick Collection) 16, 27 above, 139 above, 158; (Gift of Joe and Ruth Sataloff in honor of Susan B. Kaplan) 111 above; (Gift of John Templeman Coolidge, Jr., and others) 111 below; (Gift of Misses Cornelia and Susan Dehon in memory of Mrs Sidney Brooks) 141; (Gift of Mrs. Edward Jackson Holmes) 163 right; (Gift in memory of Mrs. Horatio Appleton Lamb) 27 below; (Gift of Mrs. Lorenz E. Ernst) 163 above left; (Museum purchase with funds donated anonymously and by Joanne A. Herman, Susan B. Kaplan, and Textile Curator's Fund) 206; Courtesy Steven Neckman, Inc. (photos Wendie Gold): 82 above, 177 right; Courtesy Nelson Rarities: 56 below left, 103 above right and below right, 147 below, 175 left; Newark Museum: (Gift of Elizabeth Reid Walker, 2000) 29 above, (Gift of Mrs Russell D. Lewis, 1941) 140, (Gift of Mrs D. H. Keller, 1926) 160 centre; Courtesy Primavera Gallery, New York: 80, 86 centre, 115 centre and below, 126 below, 144 both, 151 below; Courtesy Primavera Gallery, New York © 2010 Artists Rights Society (ARS), New York/SABAM, Brussels: 214 above; Private collection of Her Serene Highness Princess Grace of Monaco, Principality of Monaco (photo

courtesy Van Cleef & Arpels): 2–3 and 37 below right; Private collection (photos © Samuel Bristow): 172, 224; Courtesy Douglas Rosin, Chicago (photos Rebecca Uhle): 18 both, 51 below, 176 left, 177 above; Courtesy Kara Ross: 189 both; 215 above; Courtesy Anthony Roussel/Courtesy Charon Kransen Arts, New York (photos Rob Popper): 196, 197; Courtesy Pat Saling, New York: 33 above left and below; 87 left and right; 110 above left, 128 bottom left, 166; Courtesy S. J. Shrubsole, New York: above right; Collection Nick Silver, London: 213 below; Courtesy Kiff Slemmons (photo © Rod Slemmons): 211 below right; Courtesy Sotheby's, Inc.: 9, 47 both, 52, 53, 65 right, 96, 102 below, 114 below, 119, 127 both, 137, 146, 147 above, centre, and below right, 148 left and right, 173; Courtesy Sotheby's, Inc. © 2010 Artists Rights Society (ARS), New York/ADAGP, Paris: 66 above, 67; Collection Symbolic & Chase (photo courtesy Van Cleef & Arpels): 37 above right; Courtesy Taffin: 128; Courtesy Taffin and Sotheby's Diamonds by James de Givenchy: 185 left; Courtesy of Dame Elizabeth Taylor (photos © John Bigelow Taylor): 49 both, 88, 117; Courtesy 3 Ren: 185 below; Tiffany & Co.: 58 below, 187 (photo Josh Haskin), 188; Tiffany & Co. Archives: 82 below, 85, 101 below, 102 above; Courtesy Jennifer Trask: 202 all, 203 both; Courtesy 21st Century Jewels, London: 180 all, 181 both; Van Cleef & Arpels Collection: 37 left, 44 both, 68 left, 87 centre, 108 below right, 109, 175 right, 182 both, 183 both, 208 below left; Private collection (photo courtesy Van Cleef & Arpels): 31, 40 left, 41, 46; Photo courtesy Raphael Vendome: 60; Courtesy Verdura: 131, 151 above; Courtesy Verdura (photos © David Behl): 130 above, 152; 81 below (photo © 2008 Tom DuBrock); Victoria & Albert Museum, London (V&A Images): 75 right, 161, (Courtesy Geoffrey Munn) 169, 207; (Gift of Cheryl Smith through The Art Fund) 29 below; (Given by Miss Joan Hurst through the Art Fund) 124 all; Courtesy Patricia Von Musulin, New York: 8, 21, 90, 91 all, 184 centre; The Walters Art Museum, Baltimore: 205 both, 210 above, 212 below, 213 centre; The Walters Art Museum, Baltimore © 2010 Artists Rights Society (ARS), New York/ADAGP, Paris: 69, 77; Courtesy Wartski, London: 104 below, 143; Courtesy Windsor Jewelers, New York: 159; Courtesy Woodard & Greenstein American Antiques, New York: 176 left (photo Maestros de Taxco), 176 right.

The text on page 89 quotes the song 'Ebony and Ivory' by Paul McCartney, 1982.

Acknowledgments

———•————————•———

Between the genesis of a book and its completion, a network of people come together to help in the making of a book, and this publication has gathered a groundswell of people, both in America and in Europe.

For years I have admired Thames & Hudson, and over the years had opportunity to work with the house in an editorial capacity on some projects. With this book, our relationship has become one of publisher and author, and I could not be more pleased. Once Jamie Camplin, Editorial Director, expressed interest in my project I became the insider who learned firsthand what it was like to work with this great editor and his superb team. Jamie's Old World manners and keen intelligence allowed for lively exchanges and thoughtful decisions. I am grateful for his wisdom and steady encouragement. Through Jamie, I was gifted with a superb editor and designer: Amanda Vinnicombe and Avni Patel. Although they are in London and I am in New York, the distance soon dissipated and left me with a sense of camaraderie and trust – no small feat. Amanda has a keen mind and calming manner, and in the process of working together has become a friend. Avni, quite simply, is gifted. Her knowledge of design and infectious spirit are a potent reminder of Alexey Brodovitch's famous directive: 'Astonish me!' Also at Thames & Hudson, I thank Sam Ruston, Susanna Friedman, Johanna Neurath, Lisa Cutmore, and in New York, Peter Warner, formerly of Thames & Hudson, who first saw in my proposal a diamond in the rough, and sent it to Jamie for consideration. I am also indebted to Mark Magowan, publisher of the Vendome Press, New York, for bringing out my book in the United States. Mark has always had a keen appreciation of jewelry, and it is a pleasure to be part of his distinguished house.

In gathering information and photographs for this book, I had the pleasure of working with many helpful people at leading jewelry firms. My deep thanks to each: Amanda Triossi, Monica Brannetti, and Francesca Leoni, Bulgari, Rome; Susan Anthony and Ina Delcourt, Hermès, New York and Paris; Annamarie Sandecki, Lauren Turner, and Rena Gottlieb, Tiffany & Co., New York; Nicolas Luchsinger, Catherine Cariou and Cindy Prasnal, Van Cleef & Arpels, New York and Paris; Ward Landrigan, Nico Landrigan, and Caroline Stetson, Verdura, New York.

Excellence is the pursuit of the best dealers, and each of these people and their shops are exemplars of their field: Mark Schaffer, À La Vieille Russie, New York; Simon Teakle, Betteridge, Greenwich, Connecticut; Peter van Lennep, DK Bressler, New York; Gus Davis, Camilla Dietz Bergeron, and Jane Mangeri, Camilla Dietz Bergeron, Ltd., New York; Paolo Costagli, New York; Denise De Luca, de Grisogono, New York; Kristofer Bonifas, Fourtané, Carmel, California; Rebecca Selva and Karen Handley, Fred Leighton, New York; Janie Burton, Hancock's, London; Marion Harris, Marion Harris Ltd., New York; Clive Kandell, New York; Robin Katz, Robin Katz, Ltd., New York; Marcie Imberman and her son, Matthew Imberman, Kentshire Galleries, New York; Charon Kransen, Charon Kransen Arts, New York; Ben Macklowe, Macklowe Gallery, New York; Libby Cooper and Cindy Brennan, Mobilia Gallery, Cambridge, Massachusetts; Steve Neckman and Wendie Gold Karp, Steven Neckman, Inc., Miami; Malcolm Logan, Nelson Rarities, Portland,

Maine; Audrey Friedman, Primavera Gallery, New York; Barbara Rosin and Rebecca Uhle, Douglas Rosin, Chicago; Pat Saling, Patricia Saling, New York; Tim Martin, S. J. Shrubsole, New York; Nick Silver and Rona Bierrum, 21st Century Jewels, Ltd., London; Geoffrey Munn and Kieran McCarthy, Wartski, London; Avi Fattal, Windsor Jewelers, Inc., New York.

I am indebted to these museums for the excellence of their collections, curators, staff, and for providing photos: Judy Rodoe and Beatriz Waters, British Museum, London; Fashion Institute of Technology, New York; Yvonne Markowitz, Emily Banis, and Erin Schleigh, Museum of Fine Arts, Boston; Ulysses Grant Dietz and Olivia Arnone, Newark Museum, New Jersey; Joan Elisabeth Reid and Ruth Bowler, Walters Art Museum, Baltimore; Fiona Grimer, the V&A Museum, London. The auction houses were an invaluable source of images and information, and I was helped in this regard by Emily Barber, Bonham's, London, and Deborah Boskin, Bonhams & Butterfields, San Francisco; Daphne Lingon, Christie's, New York; Carol Elkins, Emily Waterfall, and Ashley Flight, Sotheby's, New York.

To the jewelers and their staffs, more thanks: Annabella Beretta and Patricia Le Caye of Anaconda, Paris and Milan; Alexia Uri, Lorenz Bäumer, Paris; Jill Burkee and Germana Pucci; Pasacale Cohen, Alexander Bittar, New York; Liv Blåvarp, Lena, Norway; Christine J. Brandt, New York; Barbara Ryan, Wallace Chan, New York; Marilyn Cooperman, New York; Paolo Costagli, New York; Jessica Kagan Cushman, New York; Karen Chan, Dior, New York; Victoria Lam, James de Givenchy, New York; Elizabeth Gage, London; Lee M. Hale, Portland, Oregon; Christian Hemmerle, Hemmerle Jewelry, Munich; JAR, Paris; Mesi Jilly, New York; Gabriella Kiss, New York; Rebecca Koven, New York; David Linley, London; Ted Muehling and Loring McAlpin, Ted Muehling, New York; Kara Ross, New York; Anthony Roussel, London; Kiff Slemmons, Chicago; Jennifer Trask, New York; Jean Vendome and Raphael Vendome, Paris; Patricia Von Musulin, New York.

A number of people offered advice, answered questions, and gave their permission to reproduce images: Craig Basmajian, Barbara Berkowitz, Françoise Cailles, Gabriella De Ferrari, Marcie Imberman, Julia Leach, Yvonne Markowitz, Tim Mendelson, Caroline Rennolds Milbank, Ana Rogers, Karen Rostenberg, Dame Elizabeth Taylor, Ingrid Thomas. Special gratitude to Laura Jacobs, who read portions of the manuscript and led me to higher ground, and always to my agent, Alice F. Martell.

Most of all, abiding thanks to my friend Daphne Lingon, senior vice president, senior specialist at Christie's, who hatched the idea for this book with me and then with unnecessary modesty remained in the wings. She is generosity personified.

R.P.
New York, New York

Index

page 221

Ivory dachshund brooch,
by Cartier, c. 1955?
Ivory, diamonds and 18K gold
As the writer H. L. Mencken said,
'A dachshund is a half-dog high
and a dog-and-a-half long.'

Bow brooch,
by Fabrice, French, c. 1990
Wood
An ingénue of a brooch – a little flirty,
a little sassy, a little innocent.

First published in the United Kingdom in 2010 by Thames & Hudson Ltd,
181A High Holborn, London WC1V 7QX

British Library Cataloguing-in-Publication Data
A catalogue record for this book is available from the British Library

ISBN 978-0-500-51533-4

Printed and bound in China by C&C Offset

To find out about all our publications, please visit **www.thamesandhudson.com**.
There you can subscribe to our e-newsletter, browse or download our current catalogue,
and buy any titles that are in print.